The issue of the human rights (
Middle East – especially Christ
painfully acute than it has been t
that raises some complex qu
framework might work best to
Avoiding simplistic solutions and .... carefully to the
agenda set by those on the front line, it provides a uniquely
thoughtful perspective.
Lord Williams of Oystermouth, Master Magdalene College
Cambridge, Archbishop of Canterbury (2003-13)

Jonathan Andrews has written an admirably clear account of
how compulsory registration of religious affiliation plays into
issues of discrimination and fuels violence throughout the
Middle East. In 2010 the European Court of Human Rights
argued that the removal of religious affiliations from identity
cards would help end discrimination while Article 18 of the
1948 Universal Declaration of Human Rights insists – along
with many religious leaders – that there must be no coercion in
religion. Jonathan Andrews' 'Baedeker's Guide' to the
countries and practices of the region includes some very
helpful ideas about how to create greater diversity, tolerance
and mutual respect. He was tasked by some of the region's
minorities to 'help us find a way through.' This objective,
constructive, and compelling narrative is his well-crafted
response.
Lord David Alton, Professor Lord Alton of Liverpool

It's time to get beyond the generalisations about Christians in
the Middle East, and there's no better way of doing this than by
wrestling with some of the human rights issues which affect the
lives of Christians in the region. One of the great strengths of
this very readable book is that it deals with each country
separately, seeking to understand how legal issues affecting the
lives of Christians have been shaped by history, religion,
politics and demography. Here is a challenge to all who want
Christians to remain rooted in the Middle East and not to
emigrate to the West. I hope it may point the way for a new

generation of activists, journalists and people with legal and sociological training – both nationals and foreigners – who are willing to work patiently and creatively for the common good within the political system in each country of the region.

Colin Chapman, visiting lecturer in Islamic Studies at the Arab Baptist Theological Seminary Beirut and formerly lecturer in Islamic Studies at the Near East School of Theology Beirut

Jonathan has done something extraordinary. He's taken the world's most complex and volatile region today – the Middle East – and examined one of its most divisive and partisan issues, individual rights and freedoms, especially religious freedom. Yet the result is this very readable and informative book, born out of his detailed and personal knowledge merged with his clarity and objective presentation that leaves you with a touch of hope. Everyone interested in the Middle East and Human Rights, from whatever persuasion, needs to read this book.

Martin, OM Middle East Partnership Champion & George Verwer, OM Founder & International Speaker

Sometimes the persecutor is a person. Sometimes the persecutor is a system. This book not only shows the brutal side of persecution, but how subtle and fierce is the myriad pressures on Christians from a Muslim Background in the Middle East today. 'Set my people free' is what Moses thundered to the Egyptian overlords. Jonathan Andrews delivers the same call, with precision and love. This sane analysis and overview is greatly needed for all God's people to flourish in the Middle East today.

Brother Andrew, author of *God's Smuggler* and Founder of Open Doors

Who are we? This is a key question for everyone, and a crucial one for people who change their beliefs. In a world of identity cards, changing to establish recognised new identities in Christ is a major struggle. Jonathan takes us on a compelling journey, examining religious identity from every angle, presenting an insightful guide to the Middle East and North Africa, revealing the realities of following Christ, and setting out the challenges governments and regimes must face.

Canon Mike Parker, International Director MECO (Middle East Christian Outreach)

Many of us in the West have little understanding of the importance of the question of identity. We are so used to making lifestyle choices and defining our own identity that it comes as a shock to realise that many people in the Middle East live under a system of Registration which effectively defines their identity for them. This carefully researched and nuanced book explores the implications of this Registration system as it is variously operated across the Middle East. The author's concern to listen to the voices of local people is particularly commendable, as is his avoidance of simplistic solutions. There is a deep challenge here for those of us in the West who want to support our brothers and sisters in this region of the world which has known so much pain and sorrow.

Rt Rev Martyn Snow, Bishop of Tewkesbury

Researcher and advocate Jonathan Andrews offers a concise, highly readable overview of how human identity in the Middle East is largely, and almost unchangeably, defined by official registration based on religion. Readers will find no simple answers, but are sure to gain a clearer understanding of this complex issue. This book should definitely be read by anyone interested in the Middle East, human rights and religious liberty issues, and understanding those who desire to follow a different faith from those in which they were raised.

David Greenlee PhD, Editor of *Longing for Community: Church, Ummah, or Somewhere in Between?* (William Carey Library, 2013) International Research Associate with Operation Mobilization, served with OM for 38 years

This is an excellent book written on a subject which affects millions of people around the world today. Changing one's religion is a right enshrined in Article 18 of the Universal Declaration of Human Rights, and yet those doing so can often face huge problems, particularly if the conversion is away from the Islamic faith. Jonathan takes us on a comprehensive and detailed tour of countries where Islam is the majority religion and by using real life stories shows us clearly both where and how registration causes problems in areas such as education, employment, marriage and even burials. This is a must read for anyone with either a working or prayerful interest in the Middle East and in the subject of conversion.

Mervyn Thomas, Chief Executive Christian Solidarity Worldwide

Religious affiliation should be freely changeable in any direction and without any legal recriminations. Apostasy should not be a crime. There should be no coercion in religion. People should also be free to change their religious registration. And religious affiliation should not be registered in identity documents in the first place. This is what international norms say. And this would reduce the abuse of power and increase freedoms.

This is the quintessence of this well written book. Jonathan Andrews' able analysis reveals that the current practice in most countries of the Middle East and North Africa is quite far from this ideal. There are rare positive exceptions in only a few countries. A historically grown system of control via ancient religious communities is shaping family law. One of the steps to alleviate this situation would be the introduction of civil marriage as a complement to religiously based procedures.

Dr Christof Sauer, Professor of Religious Studies and Missiology with a focus on religious freedom and persecution research, Evangelische Theologische Faculteit Leuven Belgium, Co-Director, International Institute for Religious Freedom, www.iirf.eu

Jonathan Andrews' book, *Identity Crisis: Religious Registration in the Middle East* is impressive and imminently relevant. The author tackles head-on the single most significant issue affecting the future of the Middle East region and of its flourishing, namely: religious registration. But rather than merely treating the latter organizing principle as a dinosaur inherited from the Ottoman era, he is able convincingly to frame it in its more profound sociological context of deeply tribal societies.

The analysis is historically thorough and thoughtful. Each country is examined in its own right, while more intrinsic communal ills are recognized, helping a more unified approach. In addition to a multitude of case studies that help illustrate the complex problems, Andrews also proposes solutions which, thanks to the post-Arab-Awakening era that we live in, stand out as not just utopian and unreachable. The core problem that he identifies as needing to be addressed is what he calls the 'pluralism deficit' that all the countries examined have in common. By emphasizing this ill, he manages to set his exploration in the more universal challenge brought in by globalization in a post-colonial world, even if the causes of this deficit in the Middle East – and hence its solutions – are different from those in other parts of the world.

Andrews' search was triggered by the call of Middle East Christians to 'help us find a way through.' Therefore the author does not stop at an impartial analysis of history and of legal facts, moving to offer very pertinent recommendations in his concluding chapter: the need for the emergence of a civil system that would complement the existing religiously-based mechanisms; a call for people's right to change their religious registration to align with their beliefs and practices; a clear rule of law applied equally and impartially to all citizens; and the decriminalization of an individual's decision to change religion – the infamous accusation of 'apostasy.'

In these closing recommendations, Andrews becomes a veritable advocate for Christians and other numerical minority groups within Middle Eastern societies. His book needs to be viewed as a solid, convincing and practical blueprint for individuals, groups and governments seeking reform and transformation. Only this sort of vision can assist in transitioning Middle Eastern countries out of the rot of injustice and backward social organization, propelling them to the place of leaders and models of ethnic and religious pluralism in a world that suffers from a dangerous deficit on both counts.

Martin Accad PhD, Director Institute of Middle East Studies Arab Baptist Theological Seminary Mansourieh Lebanon, Affiliate Associate Professor of Islamic Studies, Fuller Theological Seminary, Senior Fellow of Middle East Program, Centre on Religion and Global Affairs www.crga.org.uk

Numerous religious books have been written about every subject you can think of regarding life in the Middle East as Christian or as someone who would like to adhere to it. However, Jonathan Andrews has tackled well and with depth, one of the issues that is considered as the root cause of much of the persecutions by authorities as well as by society in general. Religious registration goes back many centuries and has brought tremendous suffering to so many people. Extensive research and studies have enabled Jonathan to put in one book illustrated by real life stories that will help every reader understand well the situation. I trust that Western as well as Middle Eastern policy makers will be motivated to use their influence to bring lasting changes to this root cause of persecution.

Henri Aoun, Director Life Agape

At a time when we badly need help in understanding the Middle East, this timely book takes us below the surface to understand the realities that shape the lives of Christians. Sympathetically, clearly and carefully, years of experience and insight are presented in highly accessible form, enabling the reader to understand the complexities of the region and how we can pray and support our brothers and sisters. I highly recommend this book.

Paul Bendor-Samuel, International Director of Interserve former chair of the North Africa Partnership (2000-02)

Identity Crisis:

Religious Registration in the Middle East

Jonathan Andrews

Gilead Books Publishing
Corner Farm
West Knapton
Malton
North Yorkshire
YO17 8JB UK
www.GileadBooksPublishing.com

First published in Great Britain, January 2016
2 4 6 8 10 9 7 5 3 1

Copyright © Jonathan Andrews 2016

British Library Cataloguing-in-Publication Data:
A catalogue record for this book is available from the British
Library.

ISBN-13: 978-0-9932090-2-4

All scripture quotations, unless otherwise indicated, are taken
from the HOLY BIBLE, NEW INTERNATIONAL VERSION.
Copyright © 1973, 1978, 1984 by International Bible Society.
Used by permission of Hodder & Stoughton, a member of the
Hodder Headline Group. All rights reserved. 'NIV' is a trademark
of International Bible Society. UK trademark number 1448790.

Quotations from the Qur'an are taken from www.quran.com.

The map of the region on page 22 was kindly supplied by Middle
East Concern (www.meconcern.org), used with permission.
Maps of Jordan, Egypt, Turkey, Iran, Iraq, Syria and Yemen were
generously supplied by the International Institute of Religious
Freedom (www.iirf.eu), used with permission.

Cover design: Nathan Ward

This book is dedicated to those across the Middle East who have endured religiously motivated persecution.

Some of these are named in this book; there are many more with similar stories.

Jonathan Andrews has been researching and writing on Middle Eastern issues since 2003.

This, his first book, looks at a deeply significant feature of Middle Eastern societies, exploring the effects on Christians, Muslims, other religious communities and society as a whole.

CONTENTS

Preface

"Helping us find a way through would be a significant contribution." I was speaking with a Middle Eastern church leader about religious registration, the system prevalent across the Middle East that identifies every human being as an adherent of a particular religion. "You see," he explained, "the system is used by Muslims to determine who should get the benefits of being part of the majority and by some Church leaders to identify Christians. However, we are only too aware of the problems it causes for those who choose to follow Jesus from Muslim backgrounds. So, we cannot simply say 'do away with the system,' but we need a solution for those who choose to become Christ's followers."

My own journey with religious registration in the Middle East began with the challenges posed to Christians. I joined Middle East Concern (www.meconcern.org) in January 2003, becoming part of a network of Christian groups and individuals seeking to support those who suffer for being or becoming Christians in the Middle East and North Africa. The first long-running case of religiously-motivated persecution that I was involved with concerned a Jordanian lady, a widow, at risk of losing custody of her two children. Later came cases in which people had been beaten, imprisoned and forced to leave their country. Then came those who initiated legal challenges seeking to modify legal systems that are rooted in religious registration. Finally, as I explored the topic came the observations of how religious registration permeates society with numerous subtle effects.

Amidst the legal cases were the discussions on the effects on people's daily lives and sense of identity. "I am a follower of Jesus, which makes me a Christian. Yet my country, my government and my society, treats me as though I am a Muslim. The government refuses to acknowledge my decision to become a Christian. There is no mechanism by which the change can be recognised because the government has refused to create such a mechanism. Indeed, society refuses to accept that such a change is possible, despite the testimony of people like me who have embraced Jesus Christ." Another noted that "at home I tell my children that we are Christians yet at school the state tells them they are Muslims. This is deeply confusing to their young minds."

It was only later that I heard of church leaders speaking positively about religious registration. "I know to whom I am a pastor, who is part of my 'flock,'" to use a religious metaphor, "and for whom I must provide due care and support." Equally, they know who is not their responsibility, at least officially, although few are willing to explicitly acknowledge this. There are reasons for such caution; I am only too aware that the political authorities in several countries discreetly inform Church leaders that there will be serious repercussions for encouraging non-Christians to attend churches. One motivation is to prevent disturbances to social harmony. Further, I've read numerous stories of mob violence against church leaders, their congregations and places of worship because those whose religious registration is not Christian have been made welcome. The photographs of the aftermath are not pretty, and physical and psychological wounds take time to heal. The whole community is affected, not just the church leaders. One consequence is the creation of tensions amongst church leaders on whether and how to interact with non-Christian neighbours.

In recent years I have become increasingly aware that so many of the challenges faced by Christians in the Middle East have at root the system of religious registration. As the church leader above noted, it separates society into the majority and the rest. This facilitates discrimination and marginalisation, with subtle effects in employment, career paths and business. It underlines the treatment of some Christian communities as second class citizens, a practice referred to as "dhimmi status" by some Muslims.

So, what actually is religious registration about? The practical effect is that it identifies which legal code applies to them for family matters such as marriage, children's education, divorce, custody of children, burial rites and inheritance. There is no civil system; everyone is obliged to use the religiously based system that matches their religious registration. Major challenges occur for those wishing to marry whose registrations are different. Most countries restrict the options for changing registration and in the few countries that have no legal restrictions, various forms of societal discrimination frequently occur. Those who choose to become adherents of another religion, i.e. converts, can face a variety of challenges, especially if they are not allowed to change their registration to match their chosen religious belief and practices.

Religious registration permeates society with consequences for everyone and society as a whole. It classifies people by their religion, or a presumption of their religious adherence based on their family background. For some it explicitly identifies them as belonging to one strand within the broad spectrum of their religion, e.g. Maronite Catholic or Eastern Orthodox within Christianity and Shi'a, Ismail or Sunni within Islam. For others, it suppresses their distinctiveness within something that they would prefer not to be identified with, for example regarding Druze or Alevi as part of Islam.

This book explores the topic, noting the effects on all parts of society. It endeavours to reflect the diversity of views that exist amongst Christians in the Middle East which range from 'hate it' to 'find it very useful.' This diversity of view underlies the challenge of finding a way through.

At the outset I need to affirm that I regard respect for the local agenda as a fundamental element of supporting those facing injustice since any adverse consequences of actions taken by those outside of the situation are likely to be borne by the victim. Therefore they – together with those close to them – must decide what course of action they will take and what support by others they desire. This affirms the dignity, intelligence and intrinsic value of the individuals concerned and respects the local agenda. I summarise this as 'informed consent' or 'informed local authorisation.' This principle is included in the Best Practice document of the Religious Liberty Partnership, which encourages and facilitates collaboration amongst Christian organisations involved in freedom of religion issues.[1] As someone who lives outside the Middle East, I wish to affirm that support of people in the region can be helpful and effective; equally we need to be aware that inappropriate actions can be unhelpful. Regrettably, I have seen too many examples of agendas planned outside the region being imposed and causing significant harm to indigenous communities.

"Help us find a way through." Thank you for the challenge and it is my privilege to ask several questions and to make a number of suggestions. The former include in what ways religious registration helps or hinders society to flourish or, using a religious and harsher metaphor, in what ways is it a blessing or a curse on the Middle East.

---

[1] See Principle 2 "Doing No Harm" in the RLP's Best Practices document;
http://www.rlpartnership.org/downloads/RLP_Best_Practices_March_2014.pdf (accessed 10th April 2015)

Acknowledgements

I have contemplated writing on the subject of religious registration since 2009 and explored it as a topic for a PhD. In 2013 a professor in the Middle East remarked that it was an important and timely topic and suggested that I consider writing a book. In 2014 the opportunity arose as I took a sabbatical from work commitments.

One constant throughout the consideration and the writing process has been the steadfast encouragement of my wife Wendy. Alongside this has been the faithful support of friends and family in friendship, faithful prayer and financial support without which this book would not be in your hands today.

I also wish to express my thanks to the many Christians across the Middle East for their time, wisdom and trust in explaining the intricacies of the cases and other matters described, as well as all too many more cases that have been omitted. Such insights continue to enrich my understanding of the complexities of the Middle East. In addition I appreciate the reading and interpretation of sacred texts when explained by nationals from the lands in which these documents originated.

I likewise express my thanks to the expatriates of many nationalities with whom I have worked during the past 15 years. I thank you for the clarifications and insights that have emerged during discussions of the underlying context.

Specific thanks go to those who have read drafts of this book (in whole or in part) and whose comments and suggestions have been helpful, including Phil Bourne, Stephen Carter, Malcolm Catto, Rob Duncan, Keith Gibbins, Tudor Griffiths, David Meakin, Mike Parker, Alison Pascoe, David Shoesmith and Mike Workman. The final text is improved because of the time and wisdom offered by each contributor. In addition, a number of those who have endorsed the book have also provided constructive comment on points of detail within the text for which I am grateful. Finally, my thanks to Chris Hayes at Gilead Books, whose expertise in publishing I have greatly appreciated.

Quotations from Marwan Muasher's book *The Second Arab Awakening and the Battle for Pluralism* published by Yale University Press in 2014 (ISBN 978-0-300-

18639-0) are used with permission from Yale University Press (London).

References to books and other writings by Martin Accad, Ron Boyd-MacMillan, Colin Chapman, Nik Ripken and jointly by Maryan Rostampour and Marziyeh Amirizadeh are used with the kind agreement of the authors.

The views expressed are those of the author; they are not necessarily those of any person or group that I have worked for or alongside.

I am aware that the book describes the religious registration system which is being adjusted in some places and challenged across the region. It is entirely possible that discreet efforts seeking change are underway, initiated by members of diverse religious groups. I apologise for any omissions on my part. The text reflects my knowledge and understanding at the time of completion, August 2015. It is my firm belief that the overall picture presented is an accurate description of religious registration in the Middle East at this time.

The region is in the throes of turmoil. My constant prayer is for true peace to be inaugurated and maintained for the benefit of all the peoples of the Middle East.

I am aware that translation always involves elements of interpretation, a fact that affects the reporting of political events, court cases, etc. I endeavour to take this into account when reading and assessing translated material.

Introduction

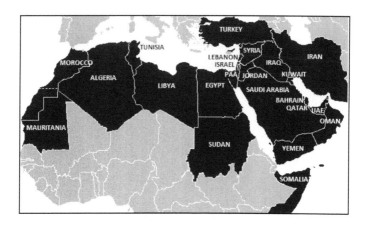

How does religious registration underpin an identity crisis in the Middle East? What are the effects of this crisis and why is it not more widely recognised? Crucially, how might the situation be mitigated?

Much of the Middle East is in a period of profound change. In many parts there are calls for greater dignity, more and better jobs and a clear voice in governance. In some parts there is conflict, turmoil and uncertainty. Amidst this changing context, what options are there for addressing the identity issues faced by so many?

In the aftermath of the removal of President Saddam Hussein of Iraq in 2003 several commentators asked,

'How many Iraqis are there in Iraq?' Their observation was that we knew (or at least had an approximate idea of) the numbers of Kurds, Sunnis, Shi'a and other ethnic-religious groups. The question was whether they saw themselves as citizens in a shared country, i.e. as Iraqis, or as members of a number of groups that would compete for influence, power and resources. There appeared to be the assumption that for one group to gain another must lose.

This assumption is rooted in the history of the area in which the overall wealth, resources and opportunities change only slowly. It needs to be demonstrated that this is false in the modern context; wealth can be generated and new opportunities created, allowing societies to flourish for the benefit of all. There are calls in the region for this and some examples of it happening.

The sense of identity and belonging comes from a variety of factors, including family, wider family, tribe, ethnicity, religious affiliation, employment/career, as well as nationality. It is a complex topic. One feature prevalent across the Middle East is the linking of religious affiliation with ethnic and tribal identity. This can create very strong communities where all members share large parts of their sense of identity.

However, it creates grounds for several challenges, one of which is for those who choose to become adherents of a different faith.

Religious registration identifies every person with a particular faith, making them part of a religiously-defined community. This identification is maintained irrespective of the individual's religious belief or practice, which prompts profound questions as to what it means to be a Muslim, Christian, and so on. Religious registration can either emphasise or suppress the different strands within the religions present in the Middle East.

The major religions in the Middle East are, in historical order, Judaism, Christianity and Islam. They share a common ancestry and several theological elements, notably being monotheistic. All three are diverse, with several major strands present in all three faiths (see appendices 1, 2 and 3 for a description of the origins of such diversity). Politics, geography and theology feature in the story of all three religions, and economics plays a part in the early history of Islam.

There have been Christian communities in the Middle East since the first century. For many, their sense of identity and belonging is rooted in long-standing churches with a defined place in society. They and their ancestors have been Christians for generations, indeed centuries. What challenges and issues do they face for *being* Christians? Is their presence wanted or resented? Leaders of several countries are overtly urging them to stay and continue contributing to society, notably economically as they own and manage a disproportionately high percentage of private businesses. The leaders are challenging the historic pattern of the emigration of Christians from the Middle East.

There are also people across the Middle East who have chosen to *become* Christians. What challenges and issues do they face? How do they view their sense of identity? How are they seen by others, especially within the communities into which they were born and where they were raised? Typically, such people strongly desire to be loyal members of such communities, to remain faithful to their parents, and their family in particular, as well as their community and country. However, all too frequently they are rejected. The sense of an identity crisis is felt by those close to those who convert, as well as the converts themselves.

We will embark on a tour of the region to explore these issues. We shall see that for all too many people, their sense of identity is being challenged. The order of our tour has been chosen based on constructing a picture of the challenges to people's sense of identity that occur. We will examine the stories of a number of individuals and families, using these as illustrations of the challenges, actual or potential, faced by many others. We will pause our tour to look at several themes and questions that we observe, and to explore the changing context. From the outset, we will be aware that religion is a major component of society.

It will quickly become apparent that religious conversion is not a one-way street; some Christians choose to become adherents of Islam. We will also note that sometimes what is presented as religious conversion is actually a change of religious registration for reasons not related to religion; common reasons are marriage and better job opportunities.

Perhaps we should pause briefly to define more clearly religiously motivated persecution because we will notice that many groups across the Middle East are victims of such practices. I use two definitions. The narrower one is "the violation of a person's or group's human rights for religious reasons." This links persecution to legal frameworks. The broader definition of "any hostility experienced because of one's identification with a religious belief or community" is more widely applicable. This includes hostility from neighbours, friends, colleagues and family members. It is more encompassing, and includes the subtle elements within cultures that contribute to religious intolerance.[2] As we shall see, numerous religious communities in the Middle East experience religiously motivated persecution perpetrated by their governments, their society, elements within society including armed groups and their family. Our tour will illustrate how religious registration is at the root of many of these challenges.

To the Western reader, born into an era when "tolerance" is understood to be an elementary part of one's culture, the individual's right to freedom of conscience, belief, religion and association with likeminded others is paramount. The state has no right to direct or limit his or her choice in such matters.

---

[2] This definition is derived from Ron Boyd-MacMillan's book *Faith that Endures* published by Sovereign World in 2006. This book is about religiously-motivated persecution of Christians worldwide.

There are many sources of the injustice experienced in the Middle East of which the religiously-motivated are but one. Possible responses fall into three broad categories summarised as 'accept,' 'resist' or 'flee.' The first action of supporting those facing injustice is to assist them in clarifying the facts of their situation, identifying and naming the source and form of the injustice and the motivation(s) of the perpetrator(s). This creates a clear statement of the situation which facilitates an assessment of the options available, starting with considering the likely consequences of quietly accepting the situation. Might it get worse, might the same be done to others or might the situation change for the better? This is the accept option. The alternative is to explore whether the injustice could be challenged, i.e. can the persecutor be presented with a statement of the effects of their actions and asked to correct the injustice? How might they react? This is the resist option. An essential element in resisting injustice is to be clear about why what is faced can be regarded as unjust; what laws, conventions or societal norms are being violated and why? Hence the first definition of religious persecution given above which directly links to the violation of human rights.

If neither the 'accept' or 'resist' options are palatable then the final option is to leave the situation. This option usually has long-term consequences and is frequently the hardest to implement. This is the 'flee' option, often referred to as relocation in religious persecution circles. As we shall see, relocation as a response to religious persecution should be regarded as the option of last resort, although there are situations in which it is the only viable option.

It is time to embark on our tour of the region. We will start in Jordan, the country where I was first introduced to religious registration. Those who regard this as a friendly Western-orientated nation are in for a surprise.

Chapter 1

Starting in Jordan

One of the first complex and long-running cases of religious persecution that I was involved with concerned a Jordanian widow, Siham, and her two children. This case concerned her widow's benefit and the custody of her children. The latter was resolved, a process which took seven years, but the state benefit payments were lost.

Siham's husband died in 1994 whilst serving abroad with the Jordanian military as part of a United Nations peacekeeping force. When Siham went to the authorities to claim her widow's benefit she was informed that her late husband had converted to Islam in 1991. The 'proof' of this was a 'conversion certificate' that had been signed by two witnesses but not by her husband – there was a small 'x' in the space for his signature. In Jordanian law, this document was valid, a fact confirmed by several court cases. (To Western eyes the absence of the subject's signature would render such a document incomplete and it would have no legal validity.)

This revelation came as a shock to Siham. Her husband had never spoken of any religious conversion. Siham and their two children were faithful members of a local church.

Siham, being a Christian, could not inherit from a Muslim. However, her children could, though being minors they could only do so through a guardian who was a Muslim. Siham asked a brother who had converted to Islam when he was 15 to act as the children's financial guardian. The brother was duly appointed but did not always pass the money to either Siham or her children.

In 1998 Siham's brother applied for full custody of the children, thereby starting a series of legal processes that would last seven years. In 1998 a court ruled in his favour on the grounds that the children's religious registration was changed to Muslim as a direct corollary of their father's conversion. As Muslim children they should not be raised by Siham who was a Christian.

Siham appealed. In February 2002 the Supreme Court upheld the decision. However, the children continued living with their mother. In January 2003 the brother went to court again to ensure the decision was enforced. A court order was issued to imprison Siham for 30 days unless she handed over custody of her children. She went into hiding.

During 2003, two court cases were initiated; one seeking to remove the estranged brother as the children's guardian, and the second in an Islamic court seeking to have the certificate of alleged conversion ruled invalid. The latter proved ineffective. However, the former succeeded, but took two years, and required numerous court hearings and several referrals from one court to another. On 3rd April 2005 a court ruled in Siham's favour, removing her estranged brother as the children's guardian. He had failed to prove his claim to have used money withdrawn from the children's trust account to buy a refrigerator for Siham. He appealed, but lost again. Further leave to appeal was denied, thus ending his involvement with the children.

Siham's lawyer advised against appointing a new financial guardian to remove any risk of another custody case developing. As a result, access to the widow's benefit paid into a trust account held by the court in favour of the children was lost. Effectively, the Jordanian government has denied the dependents of a soldier who died while serving abroad from receiving any state benefits due to them in recognition of the soldier's service to his country.

It is perhaps cold comfort that the legal battle over custody turned on a refrigerator!

Of note in Siham's story is that the Jordanian Royal Family became aware of her situation and were keen to see it resolved satisfactorily. During 2003 one member guaranteed to ensure that Siham would not be imprisoned and would retain custody of her children. The Monarchy is supportive of Jordan's Christian communities, a topic that we will return to in chapter 8.

Some Christians in the Middle East regard the Jordanian government as the best in the region when assessed in terms of the treatment of recognised indigenous Christians. In marked contrast, I regard Jordan as the worst in the Middle East in how it treats converts from Islam to Christianity within the legal system. This claim often surprises friends in the UK. So why am I of this opinion?

Consider the case of Ramzi, a convert, and his wife Muna, who is from a Christian background. Their lives, together with those of their two children, changed forever on Sunday 23rd March 2008.

On that day Ramzi was beaten by his brothers in-law and his father filed a lawsuit charging Ramzi with apostasy (leaving Islam). The father sought custody of Ramzi's children. When Ramzi appeared in court he told the judge that he had never been a Muslim, but rather an agnostic before deciding to become a Christian. The judge sentenced him to one week in jail for contempt of court. However, en route to prison he became ill due to his injuries from the beating and so was taken to hospital where he spent one night handcuffed to his bed. Later in the week he was released on bail. The family decided to leave Jordan for fear of how they would be treated by the Jordanian legal system.

Their fears were well founded. Precedent had been set in 2005 when another convert to Christianity was formally convicted of apostasy in a Shari'a court and lost all his civil rights. The court had annulled his marriage, awarded custody of the children to his wife and declared every document that he had ever signed invalid, including his car insurance, home ownership and phone contract. In legal terminology, he no longer had 'legal personality'; anybody could take his possessions as if they had found them discarded at a recycling centre and injuring him would be regarded in law in the same manner as injuring a rodent, giving total impunity to the perpetrator.

And so it happened to Ramzi and Muna after they had left Jordan. A Shari'a Court officially annulled their marriage and removed all Ramzi's civil rights, leaving him with no legal personality.

The couple spent some time in neighbouring countries where they applied for refugee status and resettlement. They were eventually able to formalise their residency in a Western country, although the process took five and a half years. Alas, such timescales are not unusual for people obliged to leave their country due to religious persecution. I will leave the issue of relocation for another time, whilst noting that they replaced the certainty of turmoil with the turmoil of uncertainty. For our purposes here, we note that the religious registration issue underlies the legal system which caused their turmoil.

For both Siham and Ramzi, it was relatives who sought to use the religious registration system, and the religiously-based court system that it gives authority to, against Christians. The state allows such a structure to exist and grants it authority over citizens. However, the state did not initiate the actions against these individuals; relatives did.

In contrast, the state did initiate problems for another family. During 2007 officials visited the home of a family of regular church members, removed their identity cards which stated they were Christians and gave them new cards stating that they were Muslims. On what grounds did they do so?

Approximately 40 years previously, when the father was a child, his family changed their religious registration from Christian to Muslim. However, the father had retained his birth certificate stating that he was Christian and, having later become a regular church member, used the birth certificate to obtain an identity card stating that he was Christian. He married a Christian and had a family all of whom were registered as Christians and treated as such by the state and the community. In 2007 the authorities discovered the change made 40 years previously, and retroactively applied it to the man and his family.

How did the family respond? They went to court, lost, appealed, lost, and appealed again. The second appeal was also rejected. The family decided to emigrate.

With Siham's children, at age 18 they were able to choose which religious registration was stated on their identity cards. This was because they were Christian at birth and whilst the father's apparent change to Muslim should, in normal circumstances, change their registration during their upbringing, they would be allowed to choose when they reached adulthood. For the previous family, it is not clear why the right of this man to choose at age 18 was not respected.

Siham's children did choose to be recognised as Christians.

We have looked at three cases of Christians facing difficulties due to religious registration. In two of these the family affected felt obliged to leave the country. Emigration of Christians, and professional people who are adherents of other religions, is a major issue across the Middle East.

Consistency in application of the law is not always apparent, a trend that has been all too common in much of the Middle East in recent decades. We shall see that this is one motivation for numerous calls for reform across the region. In Siham's case, a Supreme Court decision was not enforced. Later in our tour we shall encounter an example from another country in which a Supreme Court ruling was not implemented. In that case, a Christian was disadvantaged, in contrast to Siham's case where the non-implementation was to her benefit. We are seeing already that we need to be careful what we ask for!

Inconsistent application of law was one factor in several challenges made to the religious registration system in Egypt, the second stop on our tour of the region.

Chapter 2

Challenging System in Egypt

2007 proved to be a significant year for religious registration in Egypt. Three separate but interlinked series of court cases began. All were controversial in Egypt. Two were to end successfully during 2011. The third remains unresolved. A challenging system was itself challenged!

The first case concerned people who were Christian at birth but who had become Muslim at some point and subsequently sought to return to being Christian. The change to Muslim can occur for three different reasons. First, the deliberate, conscious choice of the individual themselves. We will come across a number of reasons why people might do this, not all of them religious. Second, as the direct consequence of someone else changing their registration. Typically, when a man changes his registration, any children are automatically switched to the same registration as their father. Third, by administrative error. This latter category ought to be easy to change but in many cases in the past it was not because local officials refused to admit to having made a mistake.

In July 2007 the Supreme Administrative Court heard an appeal submitted by Christian citizens whose attempts to legally reclaim their Christian identities had been denied. Those involved in the appeal had been involved in several cases in the lower courts. In one case a court had ruled in their favour (in April 2006) and in another against the applicants (in April 2007). This is the inconsistent application of the law, a theme that we saw in Jordan. On 2nd July 2007 the Supreme Administrative Court ordered a retrial in an

Administrative Court. Court hearings were scheduled in 2007 but postponed.

On 9th February 2008 the High Administrative Court ruled in favour of 12 Christian reconverts and instructed the Ministry of the Interior to issue identity cards stating their religious registration as Christian. However, the court stated that "ex-Muslim" should be added. At least 300 other Egyptian Christians had similar applications in progress within the legal system at that time.

Two problems emerged during March 2008. First, the government's computer system only allowed a single word in the space provided for religion, implying that the order to put "Christian, ex-Muslim" in the space could not be implemented without first amending the computer system. Although the authorities appeared to have promised to simply state the holder's religion and keep the history on file, at least one applicant had his request to change his identity card refused on the grounds that the computer system could not accommodate the change.

Second, in January 2008 a judge had asked that the Constitutional Court consider whether or not the earlier ruling to allow reconversion was constitutional. The same judge had ruled against reconverts during 2007. In March 2008 it became clear that his further intervention had delayed implementation of the High Administrative Court's ruling. The original ruling was made under Article 47 of the Egyptian civil law that covers changing information on identity cards. The Constitutional Court was asked whether the ruling was consistent with Article 2 of the constitution that declares Islam as the state religion and Shari'a as the principal source of legislation. Most Muslims interpret Shari'a as forbidding apostasy. However, some lawyers argue that the Article 2 injunction applies to legislators only, not to courts. In other words, they argue that Article 2 is applicable in the parliamentary process of drafting, revising and enacting legislation. Courts, however, should apply the legal code as stated in legislation; Article 2 of the constitution is not relevant at this point. In chapter 22 we will observe that a legal system that instructs local judges to apply Shari'a leads to inconsistency due to variations in how Shari'a is understood, interpreted and applied by judges.

The delay lasted three years, during which the number of Christians adding their names to the class-action legal case continued to rise. In April 2010 it stood at 2,814.

On 3rd July 2011 the Supreme Administrative Court ruled in favour of the Christians, stating that reconversion would be permitted upon presentation of a birth certificate stating Christian and a letter from a recognised church confirming the reconversion. The Court ruled that this judgement was valid for all citizens and individual cases should not be referred to the judiciary. The Court criticised the Minister of the Interior for not implementing the previous ruling. On 6th September 2011 50 reconverts were informed that their new identity cards would be available within two weeks. At the time of writing, no subsequent problems have been reported.

The appeal took over four years but it was successful. We might reflect on whether the political and social changes occurring in Egypt from January 2011 onwards played a role in this change to the legal rights of Egyptian Christians.

It is worth noting the requirement of a letter from a recognised church. This is our first glimpse of the linkage between religious registration and the subject of which churches have or can obtain official recognition as legal entities enabling them to provide documents to citizens that will have due legal authenticity and validity before state authorities.

The second significant legal case of 2007 concerned the twin boys of a Christian couple. In 2002 the boys' father divorced their mother, converted to Islam and married a Muslim. In 2007 he exercised his legal right to forcibly change his children's religious registration. The children's mother discovered this when informed that her sons had been moved from Christian to Muslim religious education classes at school. This was a major shock to both her and her sons. Like Siham, the mother became aware of a change in someone's religious registration through indirect means. We shall encounter this again later in our tour.

The two boys refused to complete an end-of-year Islamic class test required to progress to the next year. They took their places in the examination hall, wrote their names on the top of their answer papers, put their pens down and sat still for the remainder of the allotted time. Their mother initiated a legal case to have her sons' religious registration changed back to Christian. The first hearing was held on 2nd September 2007 but the court delayed issuing a verdict until an unspecified date after 17th November 2007, which was the date that a verdict was scheduled to be issued concerning reconverts. However, delays in that process led to delays in this case too.

The next legal development occurred on 24th September 2008. The father had applied for custody of the twins. A court ruled in favour of the father, granting him custody, despite Egyptian law stating that custody should be granted to the mother if the children are under 15. This led to the award of custody being reversed on appeal, a process that took until June 2009. However, the appeal court upheld the legal precedent that when a parent becomes a Muslim the religious registration of their children automatically changes to Muslim.

The mother's counsel challenged this, asking the Ministry of the Interior to release the twins' birth certificates stating that they were Christian, though the State had retroactively changed them to Muslim. The Ministry declined. Consequently, in March 2010 a further court case was submitted. On 14th April 2010 a court issued a ruling against the claim. An appeal was submitted.

Normally in Egypt, people are issued identity cards when they reach age 16. However, the twins' identity cards were not issued in June 2010 as they should have been due to the ongoing legal case. In 2011 an Appeal Court overturned the original ruling and in October 2011 the twins' identity cards were finally issued stating that their religious registration was Christian.

This decision followed on from that concerning reconverts. The system was effectively challenged, although again the process took four years. There were serious implications for the twins' education and the stresses of the process on those involved should not be overlooked.

The third series of court hearings was more ambitious and, at least to date, has not been as successful. On 2nd August 2007 Mohammed Ahmed Hegazy filed a court case against the authorities for refusing to legally recognise his change of religion from Muslim to Christian. This was the first such challenge to be made in Egypt. One motivation was that his wife was pregnant with their first child and the couple did not want their child's birth certificate to state 'Muslim.' The child was born in January 2008, and the couple's second child in January 2010.

There was a strong reaction by Muslim clerics against Mohammed and his lawyer. The lawyer received death threats and a lawsuit was filed against him. He withdrew from the case, whereupon the lawsuit against him was dropped. Mohammed and his wife were forced to go into hiding. The case continued to receive widespread publicity in Egypt throughout 2007 and 2008.

Court hearings were held on 2nd October and 13th November 2007 at which conservative Islamic lawyers supported the government's practice of not changing identity cards. Three further hearings were held in January 2008, culminating on 29th January when the court ruled against Mohammed, stating that "he could believe what he wants in his heart but on paper he cannot convert."[3]

An appeal was submitted but there was no progress on its consideration. In February 2010 there were suggestions that a verdict was expected in April that year. The legal process was suspended pending the outcome of the Constitutional Court ruling concerning

[3] E.g. World Watch Monitor; 31st January 2008; https://www.worldwatchmonitor.org/2008/01-January/newsarticle_5209.html/ (accessed 5th August 2015)

reconverts. When the reconvert issue was settled in 2011, there remained no progress on Mohammed's case. The justice system effectively let the case wither away.

Mohammed and his family continued to face harassment because of their loyalty to Christ. Slowly, some of the pressure subsided as this case faded from people's memories. Mohammed was able to start living more normally.

On 2nd December 2013 Mohammed came to public attention once more when he was arrested in Minya. He was using a Christian community name of Bishoy Armia Bolous. He was arrested for conducting himself as if he were a journalist when he did not have the necessary licence. On 5th December he appeared in court and prosecutors stated that the charges against him included "spying for foreign organisations, photographing vital installations, proselytizing, and inciting sectarian strife." In June 2014 he was convicted of inciting sectarian strife and sentenced to five years' imprisonment. On 20th July he was released following a successful appeal. He was arrested again almost immediately, this time on charges of defaming Islam that had been submitted against him in 2009. These claims argued that simply challenging the religious registration system was in itself an insult to Islam.

It is a moot point that Egyptian law includes a three-year statute of limitations for charges against an individual. So, these charges should have been ruled invalid immediately. The legal system continues to be applied inconsistently.

Mohammed's courage inspired a second similar legal challenge which was submitted in August 2008 by Maher Gohary. This lawsuit was treated like Mohammed's and ended in the same legal paralysis. Socially, it resulted in similar ostracism and his teenage daughter Dina's schooling was severely disrupted. In 2011 Maher and Dina were able to leave Egypt, arriving in Europe via a few months in Syria. They applied for asylum. However, they chose to stop cooperating with those seeking to assist them. At some point they returned to Egypt and stated that they had reverted to following Islam, ending the pressure against them. This statement tells us nothing about what they actually believe or how they worship.

We can note in passing that this is an example of relocation in response to religious persecution that went seriously wrong, with the long-term consequences borne by Maher and Dina. They carry some responsibility for this; so too do those who initiated their move out of Egypt and made unrealistic promises that they were unable to fulfil.

At this point we will take a pause in our tour of the region to ask some questions about religious registration: what is it about, where and why did it originate?

Chapter 3

Where is Religion in Religious Registration?

At this point, let us pose a few questions about religious registration.

First question: 'Where is religion in religious registration?' Religious practice and religious belief do not feature. The ruling in the Mohammed Hegazy case shows clearly the distinction between belief – "in his heart he can believe whatever he wants" – and registration – "but he will always be regarded as a Muslim." Belief and registration are not linked. In Siham's situation, there was no evidence that her late husband ever practised as a Muslim. This fact was treated as immaterial within Jordan's legal system with regard to the change of his religious registration.

Second question: 'If religious registration is not about religious belief and practice, what is it about?' Within society religious registration determines which legal code applies to each individual on family law matters such as marriage, children's education, divorce, custody, burial and inheritance. Such matters are handled according to the traditions of the different officially recognised religions. There is no such thing as a civil marriage, all are instituted using religious rites. Islamic Shari'a, Christian canon law and Jewish Halakha law determine the personal status laws that apply to the respective communities.

This is overly simplistic. Within all three faiths there is a diversity of traditions and denominations, and a diversity of views as to how sacred texts should be interpreted and applied today. Appendices 1, 2 and 3 give a summary of how this diversity arose; politics, geography and theology feature in the story of all three religions.

Within Christianity, in the Middle East there are churches belonging to the Eastern Orthodox, Oriental Orthodox, Catholic and Protestant traditions and within each tradition there are several denominations. So, for Christian communities the major church denominations operate a system of courts that handle marriage, etc. Likewise there are religion-based courts for Muslim, Jewish and other communities. One challenge emerges when two people wish to marry but have different religious registrations. Which court system is applicable?

This prompts our third question: 'What changes are possible and how are they made?' In most Middle Eastern countries, one can change one's registration to Muslim but not from it. The two exceptions are Turkey and Lebanon. As we shall see in chapters 5 and 6, social challenges often occur for those who exercise their legal right to change their registration from Muslim.

Next question: 'So how can we summarise the problems that religious registration causes, especially for converts?' Challenges occur with marriage, raising children, religious education in schools, divorce, alimony and custody, burial rites, inheritance and oaths of allegiance. Religious registration underpins the legal definition of apostasy, i.e. leaving Islam.

Mohammed Hegazy and his wife's concern was the raising of their children. They could marry because both had religious registration as Muslim although they were forced to have a ceremony conducted according to Islamic rites. Siham's situation concerned inheritance and custody of her children. Ramzi and Muna's situation also focussed on custody of their children.

The word 'convert' merits a brief reflection. In sociological terms, the word is well defined as meaning the adoption of a religious belief and associated practices not held previously. This excludes any reference to what happens after death. One common element of religions is the view that human existence survives death in some form. We will return to this in chapter 13. Here, we simply note that the term 'convert' ignores this aspect of religion; 'conversion' is about beliefs and practices in the here and now. Within Christian circles, the word 'convert' is often heard as meaning that someone has become like us. Well, yes in some ways, maybe in others and probably not in others. *Yes*, in terms of their status before God. *Maybe*, in terms of they will worship like we do and their understanding of God as Father, Son and Holy Spirit will be similar to ours. Christianity is diverse and they may find that their preferred style of worship is amongst a different tradition to that of the first Christians they worship amongst. *No*, in terms of their socio-economic situation, life history, ethnic and national origin being unchanged. In the Middle East there are often cultural differences between Christian and Muslim communities, as well as religious differences. For converts, these cultural differences can be significant, as we shall discuss in chapter 17.

Finally: 'Where does religious registration originate?' Our initial answer to this is from the Ottoman Empire's Millet System. However, the Millet System predates the Ottoman Empire and indeed the rise of Islam. Its history can be traced to the fourth century. We will explore this further in the next chapter.

Before that, we pause to note that the use of religious courts for matters of personal status, as necessitated by the religious registration system, implies that both national and religious legal systems operate. National law covers the penal code, i.e. criminal matters, and the civil code, i.e. disputes between citizens. Religious law covers personal status, i.e. marriage, children, divorce, alimony, custody, burial rites and inheritance. Conflicts can occur when religious law attempts to operate in areas that should be the remit of national law. Typically these originate from religious law informing the moral outworking of a person's faith in daily life. We will see an example of this in chapter 14.

Chapter 4

The Millet System

Looking back in time through the history of the Middle East it can be seen that the nation states of today emerged only during the twentieth century. Prior to 1914, the Ottoman Empire controlled much of the region. Appendix 4 gives a brief summary of Middle Eastern history in the twentieth century.

Within the Ottoman Empire, there was a system which specifically referred to the separate legal courts pertaining to personal law under which minorities were allowed to conduct family matters with little interference from the Ottoman government. This system was the Millet System.

Movement of people amongst these diverse groups was discouraged, both by the authorities and the groups themselves. The rulers were keen to preserve social harmony, and to avoid conflict between different groups. Most groups were also keen that marriage was arranged between people within the same group so that dowries and subsequently inheritance kept assets within their community. Economic change was slow, with limited prospects of significant change for most which led to the culture of preserving and maintaining what assets a group owned. We will return to this theme, notably in chapter 10 as we look at some recent developments under the heading of "the Arab Awakening."

The Millet concept pre-dates the establishment of the Ottoman Empire. The earliest recorded use is in the fourth century when it was applied to the communities of the Church of the East under the Sassanid Persian Empire. This empire's state religion was Zoroastrianism. The Christians formed the Church of the East, whose leader, referred to as the Catholicos or Patriarch of the East, was responsible to the Persian king for the Christians within the Empire. This is prior to the founding of Islam. At its zenith, the Sassanid Empire's territory included much of the Middle East and those parts of the Arabian Peninsula along the Gulf and Indian Ocean coasts.

This system of maintaining Christians as a protected religious community continued after the Islamic conquest of the Sassanids in 651 AD. The Christian community flourished and was able to send people to China and India to spread the good news of Jesus' love and sacrifice.

The term 'millet' is derived from the Arabic word 'millah' meaning nation. This is not 'nation' in the modern sense of a nation state defined by its geographic territory and its capital. Instead, it is 'nation' in the historical sense of a distinct community of people sharing a language, culture and religion, and living in a loosely defined area. There were no lines on maps and, if we go back far enough, few (if any!) maps on which to draw lines! The Millet System has both Persian/Iranian and Arab origins.

Under this system, those communities that were recognised as distinct could run their own affairs in areas of family matters such as marriage, children, divorce and inheritance, as well as in some matters of local governance. Ottoman law did not recognise ethnicity or citizenship. Millets were defined solely by religion. Consequently, all Muslims of any ethnic or linguistic background throughout the empire enjoyed the same rights and privileges. The Ottoman rulers followed Sunni Islam and gave no official recognition to other forms of Islam; adherents of Shi'a Islam and adherents of Islam-derived beliefs such as the Alawites and Alevis (whom we shall meet during our regional tour) were regarded as part of the one Muslim millet. The one exception was the Druze, who had feudal-type autonomy, even if it was not an officially recognised millet – they too were part of the Muslim millet. The Druze lived in geographically definable areas, whereas the other groups were more dispersed, united by their faith – i.e. their religious beliefs and practices – but not their geography.

Ethnically and linguistically the empire was diverse, with Turkish, Arabic, Kurdish, Albanian and numerous Caucasian languages all being spoken. Likewise, today there are numerous dialects of Arabic spoken along with seven distinct Kurdish dialects. The Ottomans tried to unite these peoples under the banner of Islam. However, tensions along ethnic, linguistic and geographic lines were appearing long before the empire ended in the twentieth century. Under the Ottomans there were a number of other millets for non-Muslim religious groups. These could handle affairs within their own group. However, they had no jurisdiction in any matter where one of the parties was a Muslim. One millet was for the Jews, allowing them considerable administrative and legislative authority within their communities. This millet was represented by the Hakham Bashi, i.e. Chief Rabbi, who had access to the Sultan.

Interestingly, the Millet System used the ethnic term Jew rather than the religious term, Judaism. This is an exception to the Ottoman's general practice not to identify ethnicity. It remains the case that most Jews are followers of Judaism, some nominally and others devoutly. Some non-Jews choose to become adherents of Judaism although the religion limits their membership of the faith community. Also, some Jewish people choose to become adherents of other faiths, something we shall explore in chapter 14.

There were several millets for the Christian communities. The exact configuration changed during the history of the Empire. Initially there was one millet, the 'Rum Millet,' whose name is derived from the Romans. The Ecumenical Patriarch of the Eastern Orthodox churches, based in Constantinople, now Istanbul, was recognised as the leader of the Christian communities. There was some recognition by the authorities of the ethnic differences amongst the Christian communities which was reflected in the names of numerous churches, many of whom had their senior bishop or Patriarch. These leaders recognised the Ecumenical Patriarch as 'the first amongst equals,' in that it was he who represented everyone before the Sultan, but he had no direct authority over his fellow senior leaders. In a word, the Eastern Orthodox churches are autocephalous.

Over time, the Sultan granted the requests of different groups to be granted recognition as distinct groups with their own millets. For example, initially, the Armenian millet covered all Armenians irrespective of whether they were members of the Armenian Apostolic Church, the Armenian Catholic Church or the Armenian Protestant Church. However, separate millets were granted recognising the different churches. Other millets also came to be recognised, including the Syriac Apostolic Church of Antioch and all the East, the Chaldean Catholic Church, the Syriac Catholic and the Church of the East – who featured in the first recorded use of a millet-like system under the Sassanid Persian Empire.

There is a sharp contrast in the history between Muslims – one millet for all – and Christians – the emergence of multiple millets. Is diversity within a religion to be celebrated or lamented? Is it a strength or a weakness? We might ask whether some Christians might envy Muslims being all treated as one. Do some Muslims envy the Christians, since they would like to be recognised as distinct within a wider community but are prevented from doing so? In one country in the Middle East, namely Lebanon, the diversity within Islam has been recognised within the country's religious registration system.

We noted that the concept underlying the millet system predates Islam. To summarise, within a political entity, an empire or a nation, religious communities distinct from the faith of the rulers could enjoy protected status and administer some of their own affairs and those of their members. This is respectful and welcoming of diversity, and it allows people to mark the key transitions in life using the religious rites of their choice, with the consequent changes in personal status being duly noted by state authorities. The system is about good administration performed respectfully; it is not about control.

Islam has included such a concept, specifically as it relates to Christians and Jews, sometimes referred to as 'people of the book.' But how this has been expressed in practice varies. Across the sweep of history, tolerance and acceptance are the dominant themes, although periods of severe repression and violent attack have occurred. Christian history shows a similar pattern of periods of violence against members of other faiths or of different traditions within the same faith. Within Islam, the term 'dhimmi' is sometimes used for those not of the Muslim millet. It is often heard today as meaning second class. I sometimes question how accurate this is. There is great diversity within Islam, making categorical assessment inappropriate.

Of note here is that Christians in at least one Middle Eastern country have asked that Western Christians never describe them as a minority community. One Syrian church noted that "If you look closely enough, no ethnic-religious group is a majority." In the West, a minority is, technically speaking, a group comprising less than half the total population, although in practice it usually implies that the group is a small percentage of the population, i.e. in single figures. In the Middle East, the term 'minority' is sometimes equated with dhimmi or second class; respect can be lacking, hence the request to not use the term.

Religious registration emerged during periods of history with limited social, economic and geographic mobility. Most people lived their whole lives close to where they were born. Exceptions to this pattern were rare, in spite of well-established trade routes. One question we will address in chapter 28 is how the concept of religious registration fits with a modern age of much greater mobility. Urbanisation is one global trend profoundly affecting the Middle East.

We will resume our tour, keeping alert for similarities and differences from the Ottoman era. Our next visit is to Turkey, where we ask whether it is a modern state or an Ottoman legacy. There is no simple answer to this.

Chapter 5

Turkey – modern state or Ottoman legacy?

Turkey bridges two continents, linking Europe and Asia. The major city of Istanbul resonates with history and commercial vitality. The government led by Prime Minister Recep Tayyip Erdogan from 2002 to 2014 portrayed itself as a model of democracy and economic development under the leadership of a party with Islamic origins. Is it a model for the Middle East? What remains of the Ottoman era?

At the time of writing, Turkey's political scene appeared to be at a point of transition. In August 2014 Recep Tayyip Erdogan was elected as President. The party he leads lost its overall parliamentary majority in an election held in June 2015 and another election appeared imminent. This party has dominated parliament and the political sphere since 2002, during which Turkey has seen significant economic progress. There has been less progress in social matters, notably those which are our focus.

The state is officially a secular state, which is commonly understood to mean a state in which political decision making is independent of religious authority. In such states, political leaders are often adherents of a particular religion with some degree of religious practice. As such, their religious faith will inform their attitudes, values, behaviour and decision making.

One of the founding principles of modern Turkey in 1923 was the separation of state and religion. It was noted at that time that the state must control religion to prevent religion from controlling the state. To this day there is an innate tension between state and religion.

The state's founding document, the Lausanne Treaty of 1923, recognises the presence of a number of religious communities in addition to Muslims. These are the Armenian, Syriac and Greek Orthodox

Christians, and Jews. To be strictly accurate, the Treaty does not name these minorities but was understood to mean this list when it was written and has consistently been interpreted to refer to these religious groups.

One tension between the state and religious groups concerns the Alevi, whose beliefs combine primarily heterodox Shi'a Islamic teaching with pre-Anatolian shamanistic Turkic cultural and religious practices. Some Alevis and some Sunni Muslims do not consider the Alevi to be part of Islam. The government recognises the Alevis as an Islamic sect (a "cultural treasure"), but refuses to grant legal status to Alevi places of worship, known as Cemevi, probably because it would place both Alevis and their worship on a par with orthodox Sunni Muslims and Sunni mosques.

The Alevi are a sizeable community, commonly estimated as between five and 12 million, approximately 7-17% of Turkey's population, although a few sources state 15 to 20 million, approximately 20-30%. Variation in the available demographic data suggests that government data gathering does not distinguish amongst Sunni, Alevi and other Islamic traditions.

During the Ottoman period, the Alevi were treated as part of the Muslim millet. This practice has been continued. The diversity within Islam in Turkey continues to have only limited legal recognition from the state.

There is growing political engagement amongst the Alevis. One consequence has been their continuing efforts to gain exemption for their children from compulsory religious education in schools that teach Sunni Islam. But, as we saw in Egypt, parental choice in the religious education of children is not being honoured or respected. Having exhausted legal avenues to pursue this in Turkey, the Alevi submitted a case to the European Court of Human Rights, which ruled in their favour during 2007[4], but the government has chosen not to change the current practice; the court's ruling has effectively been ignored. This introduces the subject of the relative roles and authority of national and international law, and how national governments respond to rulings by

[4] The case was Hasan and Eylem Zeng versus Turkey (No. 1448/04) with the judgement dated 9th October 2007. www.echr.coe.int/Documents/CLIN_2007_10_101_ENG_827937.pdf, page 31 (accessed 23rd February 2015)

international bodies, a topic that we will explore further in chapter 26.

The Alevi have also taken legal action in an attempt to have Cemevis officially recognised as places of worship with consequent exemption from utility bills as is the case for mosques. Here too they went to the European Court of Human Rights, which on 2nd December 2014 ruled that the government's failure to grant this exemption violated two Articles of the European Convention on Human Rights. The government ignored this ruling too. Those running at least one Cemevi decided to stop paying their electricity bill. The electricity company took them to court, whereupon a Criminal Court ordered the immediate payment of the outstanding bills. An appeal was submitted. On 17th August 2015 the Supreme Court of Appeal ruled in favour of the Cemevi's owners on the grounds that this was clearly a place of worship and the government could not discriminate on religious grounds. If mosques are exempt, then Cemevis must be also.[5] At the time of

[5] Freedom of Belief Initiative; 18th August 2015;
http://inancozgurlugugirisimi.org/en/media/high-court-exempts-cemevis-from-paying-bills-ending-decades-long-discrimination/;
(accessed 22nd August 2015)

writing, the government's response to the ruling had not been issued.

The Alevi continue to seek representation in the Religious Affairs Directorate, which collects taxes from every Turkish citizen but only funds the activities of Sunni Islam. The state is favouring one form of Islam over other traditions within Islam and over all other religions. As we noted at the start of this chapter, there is a complex relationship between state and religion in Turkey, despite it being self-declared as a secular state.

One effect of such attention to minorities has been to prompt consideration of what it means to be *Turkish*. Clearly many people have Turkish nationality but are not ethnically Turks, with many being Kurdish or Caucasian. Turkish Kurds originate in the south-eastern parts of the country. In recent decades many have migrated to Istanbul and other western parts seeking better jobs. Intermarriage with ethnic Turks has become common, with one recent estimate being that one in six Kurds in the west of the country is married to a Turk. Kurdish communities in the south east continue to strive for greater recognition and use of Kurdish languages in education and official processes.

Identity cards issued to Turkish citizens continue to state the holder's religion. Citizens can ask for whichever religion they wish to be stated. However, the choice is limited to one of a defined list, namely Muslim, Greek Orthodox, Christian, Jew, Hindu, Zoroastrian, Confucian, Taoist, Buddhist, no religion or other. Since 2006 the space may be left blank. The process involves applying at a police station and the new card is issued promptly.

The legal situation is straightforward, even if some, notably the Alevi, cannot obtain the registration that they would like. Societal norms and expectations continue to be significant, with many people who convert choosing not to change their identity cards because of the risk of being discriminated against in job applications and official processes.

An example of this occurred during 2011 when a Christian was buried in a Muslim cemetery using Islamic rites. She had been born into a Muslim family giving her a religious registration at birth of Muslim and had decided not to change her identity card due to fear of adverse discrimination. Her will stated that she wished to be buried using Christian funeral rites but her identity card, and not her will, proved decisive in determining the burial rites used.

On 18th April 2007 three Christians, Necati Aydin, Uğur Yuksel and Tilmann Geske, were murdered at the book distribution warehouse where they worked in Malatya. Uğur was killed because of his Christian faith but was not accorded a Christian burial. According to Islamic burial tradition, females, including his fiancée, were obliged to watch from a distance. His father did insist on a Christian epitaph on the gravestone on his grave despite it being in a Muslim cemetery. On the seventh anniversary of his murder a Christian service was held at Uğur's gravesite with some of his relatives present. We will explore the events surrounding the murder of these three Christians in chapter 20.

These examples introduce the fact that some Turkish citizens with a religious registration of Muslim have chosen to become Christians. Some attend churches belonging to those Christian churches recognised in the Lausanne Treaty. Others choose to form new churches, many of which identify themselves as Protestant.

Incidentally, Istanbul remains the seat of the Ecumenical Patriarch of the Eastern Orthodox family of churches. The government recognises him only as head of his own church, The Greek Orthodox Church, also known as the Eastern Orthodox Church. The term 'Greek' here is used in the ethnic sense, not as a nationality. There are now less than 3,000 members, and they regard themselves as part of the Orthodox community along with Armenian and Assyrian Orthodox. The state refers to them as *"Rum,"* which is a continuation of the term used by the Ottoman's Millet System. The small number of members creates a serious problem in finding suitable candidates for senior positions.

Some church leaders are considering how they and their communities should think of themselves. They are encouraging Christians not to think of themselves as minorities, struggling to maintain their existence amidst overwhelming numbers of those who are different from themselves. Instead, they should regard themselves as distinct communities whose presence enriches the whole of society.

In February 2013 the Head of the Legal Committee of the Association of Protestant Churches informed the then Prime Minister Erdogan that there were 5,000 Turkish Protestant Christians. He was included in a meeting with the visiting German Chancellor at the express request of Chancellor Merkel. The association's membership comprises approximately

40 Protestant congregations. Most worshippers in these churches are from Muslim backgrounds, the others being former members of traditional churches and expatriates. Not all Protestant churches choose to join the association.

Some Protestant churches seek to register as a legal entity, one motivation being to acquire property for use as a place of worship. They are able to register as *associations*, giving them legal status as an entity but not as a religious body. Legal recognition as a religious body would bring significant further benefits, including free utilities such as electricity and water.

Some churches have been told to produce a list of people with religious registration of Christian as part of the application process for the church to gain status as a legal entity. This creates a tension for some, as encouraging church members to change their registration to support the church's application risks causing problems for them in their relationships with their families and employers.

Some small changes have been made to the religious registration system recently. We noted that since 2006 the religion section of the identity card may be left blank. It had been announced during 2004 that official documents would no longer refer to religious affiliation. Alas, when legislation supposedly designed to implement this commitment was passed in April 2006 it merely included the option of leaving the space blank. Critics noted that this barely touched the problem, since anyone who chose this option would be asked why, leading to possible discrimination.

On 2nd February 2010 the European Court of Human Rights suggested that Turkey should remove religious affiliation from its citizens' identity cards. The intention was to end discrimination based on forcing disclosure of beliefs or attracting undue scrutiny by leaving the field blank. The Court ruled that being able to leave the field blank was inadequate provision for those not wishing to be forced to disclose their faith. The case was brought by an Alevi who chose blank rather than Muslim.[6] At the time of writing, there has been no progress on implementing this ruling. This is a further example in Turkey of the non-

---

[6] The case was Sinan Işık v. Turkey, 2010-I, details of the judgement are available at
http://www.echr.coe.int/Documents/CLIN_2010_02_127_ENG_8704
55.pdf pages 15-16, (accessed 26th February 2015)

implementation of an international ruling, a subject that we will address in chapter 26.

A subtle aspect of the identity card system was exposed during 2013. In July that year a citizen of Armenian origin attempted to register her child at an Armenian kindergarten only to be told by the school to prove that she has the "2 code." When she enquired as to what was meant by the "2 code" the attendant stated that the government had included an ethnic coding system on identity cards and other official documents. The Ministry of Justice subsequently confirmed the system, which identifies Greeks (code 1) and Jews (code 3), as well as Armenians (code 2). There are concerns in many communities that government officials use the codes to discriminate against them concerning job applications, promotions, licenses and building permits. Strictly speaking this concerns ethnicity but in this context there is a clear link between ethnicity and religion, since Greeks and Armenians are presumed to be Christian and Jews to be adherents of Judaism.

Ostensibly, the government seeks to prevent religious extremism. For example, it does not permit religious meetings in homes for fear that Islamic extremism leading to religiously motivated acts of violence may originate in such meetings. Yet, religious education in schools is always from a Sunni Muslim perspective and often denigrates Alevis, non-Sunni Muslims, Jews and Christians. This is the motivation for the Alevi community to seek permission to withdraw their children from such classes. In the curriculum religious tolerance is not broadly endorsed.

In October 2006 two Turkish Christians, Hakan Taştan and Turan Topal, were charged under Article 301 of the Turkish Penal Code because of their Christian activities. At that time, this law criminalised "insulting Turkishness," a concept that was not well defined. In 2008 the law was amended to criminalise "insulting the Turkish nation," a phrase that is likewise open to different interpretations. Article 301 remains on the statute book although the number of cases has declined steadily since 2009. Since 2008 the process has been that cases must be referred to the Justice Ministry. Only those that the Ministry approves can proceed to court. In the years 2009 to 2012 the Ministry allowed less than six percent of submitted cases to proceed.

Hakan and Turan were detained briefly and released on bail. Their trial was protracted and attracted some international attention. On 14th October 2010, four years after being charged, the judges announced that they had been acquitted of "insulting Turkishness" and "insulting the Turkish nation" but convicted them of collecting data illegally. The latter related to their involvement with a correspondence Bible Study course. The judges announced a sentence of a short prison term but changed this to a fine of 4,500 Turkish Lira (approximately US$3,170). Hakan and Turan appealed, primarily to prevent a precedent being established. The Turkish courts rejected their appeal. Consequently, they submitted a case to the European Court of Human Rights. At the time of writing their case awaits a hearing.

For Hakan and Turan their decision to become Christians was viewed by their country as an insult to the nation's sense of identity, i.e. it challenged the presumption that all Turks are Muslims. It is but one example of the government regarding those citizens who are Christians, whether recognised as such by their religious registration or not, as a potential threat to the state.

As we shall see, Turkey is not the only country where Christians' loyalty to the state is questioned simply because they are registered as Christian. Christians are comfortable with their identity even if their presence causes concern or a crisis for the authorities.

Turkey is currently building a third bridge in Istanbul across the Bosporus. In May 2013 the government announced that it will be called "Yavuz Sultan Selim Bridge." Selim 1 was the Ottoman Sultan from 1512 to 1520. He expanded the Ottoman Empire into Syria, Egypt and Saudi Arabia before confronting the Safavid dynasty in Iran, who were Shi'ites. It was Selim 1 who first claimed to be Sultan of the Empire and Caliph of all Muslims. Some commentators regard the choice as evidence for describing Turkey's foreign policy as 'neo-Ottomanism.'

In Turkey we have seen that religious registration remains in force with limitations on which denominations of major faiths are recognised. An individual may change their registration but societal pressures make the decision to change a complex balance. Further changes to the laws concerning religious registration are being sought, and the Alevi religious community and Kurdish ethnic community are seeking greater respect and recognition of their distinctiveness. Many Christians would like a change of attitude by the authorities to embrace and respect religious diversity, with consequent improvement in the social acceptability of Christians and churches, as well as other religious communities.

So is Turkey a modern state or an Ottoman legacy? The treatment of non-Sunni Muslim religious communities is far from what one would expect in a modern state. Some of the suspicion with which Christians are regarded by society in general and the authorities in particular has historical origins in the demise of the Ottoman Empire.

Our regional tour takes us next to Lebanon, the other country in the Middle East that allows its citizens to change their religious registration. It is also a country where religious registration has very strong links to the political system.

Chapter 6

Lebanon – religion and politics intertwined

Lebanon is unique within the region. It is the only Arab country without a desert. It is sometimes described as the Switzerland of the Middle East; at some times of the year one can go skiing in the mountains in the morning and drive to the coast to go swimming in the Mediterranean in the afternoon.

Lebanon continues to operate a religious registration system which is directly linked to the political system. There are eighteen possible registrations for each citizen, the highest in the region. Of these, twelve are Christian, four are Muslim, one is Druze and one Jewish.

Unlike the Ottoman Empire, Lebanon distinguishes amongst different Islamic traditions. The four Muslim registrations are Sunni, Shi'a, Alawite and Ismaili. The Ismaili, sometimes called 'Sevener,' are a branch of Shi'a Islam. Likewise, so are the Alawite, although some regard them as outside of true Islam. In Lebanon, the major Shi'a denomination is the Ja'afari, also known as the 'Twelver.' (See appendix 3 for a brief description of the origins of diversity within Islam.)

Lebanon has a designated leader of its Muslim communities, 'The Mufti of the Republic of Lebanon.' The incumbent, presently Sheikh Abdel Latif Deria elected in August 2014, is a Sunni Muslim. Following his appointment he spoke movingly of the need to end violence amongst Muslim communities.

Of the twelve Christian registrations, the Maronite community is numerically the largest. It maintains a centuries long affiliation with the Roman Catholic Church but has its own patriarch, liturgy and ecclesiastical customs. The second largest is the Greek Orthodox.

Other Christians are spread amongst Greek Catholics, Armenian Orthodox (also known as Gregorians), Armenian Catholics, Syriac Orthodox (also known as Jacobites), Syriac Catholics, Assyrians (Nestorians), Chaldeans, Copts, evangelicals (including Baptists and Seventh-day Adventists), and Latins (i.e. Roman Catholic).

Lebanon has a legal process by which individuals can change their registration. To do so, a citizen must present a letter of welcome issued by the religious order or denomination that they wish to join. Legally and administratively the process of changing a person's registration works well although family and social harassment is experienced by some. This happens for converts to Christianity from other faith backgrounds, and also for some who change from one Christian tradition to another. Some regard such harassment as a mark of commitment to the change they have made and endure the harassment; others do not see re-registration as an issue and on changing their faith they retain the registration they were assigned at birth.

Religious registration is not stated on identity cards, although it is recorded within government computer systems.

A curious feature is that some government issued documents describe Lebanese Jews as 'Israelite.' The Jewish community is very small in number.

We noted above that the Druze have their own millet whereas in most Middle Eastern countries they are treated as part of the Muslim millet. It is common for Druze who choose to become Christian to leave their religious registration as Druze. They do so to affirm their continuing allegiance to their ethnic community, regarding the registration as primarily ethnic. When two such people wish to marry they fulfil the legal requirements in a Druze court and then have a religious ceremony in a church. Similarly, for burial there is a religious ceremony in a church prior to internment in a Druze community cemetery. This illustrates that for some, their religious registration is primarily an ethnic identification.

A moment of decision occurs as and when people with different registrations wish to marry. Marriage within Lebanon is exclusively within religiously based systems. In many cases, the marriage can be performed under the registration of either spouse. One exception is that a woman with a registration of Sunni can only marry a man with the same registration. In such cases, one of the intending spouses must first change their registration. An alternative option is to marry abroad and the marriage is recognised by the state.

One prompt for some to change their registration is that they are seeking a divorce. Some religious groups do not allow divorce, which forces anyone of that registration wishing to divorce to first change their religious registration.

Religious registration is embedded in the political system. The President must be a Maronite Christian, the Prime Minister a Sunni Muslim and the speaker of the Parliament a Shi'a Muslim. The Deputy Prime Minister and also the Deputy Speaker must be Greek Orthodox Christians. Being precise, these are the religious registrations that the post holders are required to hold whatever their religious beliefs and practices are. The most recent formalisation of this arrangement is the Taif Accord of 1989. This was the result of negotiations mediated by Saudi Arabia that attempted to bring the Lebanese Civil War to an end. This civil war is commonly dated as 1975 to 1991 although there were some clashes in 1974.

The Taif Accord modified some of the provisions of the constitution adopted on 25th May 1926 when the country was under a French Mandate established in the aftermath of the collapse of the Ottoman Empire. The principal change was to adjust the balance of powers amongst the President, Prime Minister and Speaker, primarily to strengthen the role of the Speaker and increase the powers of the Prime Minister at the expense of the President.

Many Christians argue that the Taif Accord was unfair towards them because it forced the Christian community to cede significant political influence with the lessening of the powers of the President. A second grievance is that one Christian political leader, namely General Aoun, was excluded from the talks, unlike senior leaders from other armed groups. He was in exile at the time, only returning in May 2005.

It remains the case that half the 128 seats in parliament are reserved for Christians and the other half for Muslims. In this division, the Druze are classed as Muslim despite having a distinct millet. This allocation is increasingly seen as biased. The religious demographics of Lebanon are much debated, with different sources providing different breakdowns. The Taif Accord can be viewed as an attempt to better align political power with the religious demographics.

At independence in 1943 Lebanon was assumed to have a Christian majority. 'Assumed' since the most recent census was taken in 1932. Similarly, accurate and agreed demographic data is not available today. This underpins the debate on what the balance is amongst the major religious groups within society. Most agree that the Shi'a have become the most numerous group, often stated as approximately 40%. Some give an approximate balance between

Christians and Sunni Muslims; others state that the Christian community is larger. There are sizeable Druze and Alawite communities, which is one reason that they have their own millets. Some demographic sources are based on electoral registers. These only list people aged 21 and above, and not the whole of the population. Consequently, they under-represent the Shi'a who typically have a higher birth rate than do the Sunni or Christian communities.

Another complication is defining what is meant by "population." It is not uncommon for Lebanese to work abroad, for example in the Gulf states, leaving their families in Lebanon and visiting regularly. They do this for financial reasons and because of the high standard of education in Lebanon which they desire for their children. This is disproportionately the case amongst Christians, followed by Sunnis. One trend in 2015 was a number of people applying to change their religious registration from Shi'a to Sunni motivated by their desire to seek work in the Gulf. Some Gulf states had become more sensitive to the religious identity of migrant workers from other Arab countries. This is a second example (after divorce) of a change of registration for non-religious reasons.

The confessional basis for the political system has been challenged by some Lebanese with calls for what they view as a modern system of constituencies of roughly equal size with no restrictions, mandates or quotas for any group within society. Most analysis of such debate indicates that it is the Christian community leaders who are most resistant to such change. They fear the erosion of their political power and influence. This fear assumes that citizens would only vote for candidates from their own ethnic-religious grouping, or their own 'tribe.' In chapter 18 we shall see an example where Middle Eastern electors have cast votes in favour of someone from a different ethnic group because they approved of the competent manner in which the incumbent was governing their city.

It was in Lebanon that my own understanding of religious registration was broadened. The status quo is appreciated by some within the Christian communities, although some Church leaders use it as a control mechanism occasionally. For example, one church member was told that if he did not act in accordance with the priest's wishes then the church would refuse to conduct a wedding service for his daughter. Religious registration was thus being used as a social control mechanism, exploiting the absence of civil marriage and the social implications for those who change their registration.

We noted in our review of the history of religious registration that the intention was to respect diversity and difference, not to be a control mechanism. Here is an example of a human system intended for good purposes being twisted, abused and contorted to facilitate those in power exerting undue control over others.

In Lebanon, we have noted that there are 18 distinct registrations, the respect for diversity within Islam, allowing more Muslims to use rites of passage specific to their beliefs and practices, and the direct linkage to the political system. The next stop on our regional tour will be a second visit to Jordan which also has interaction between its religious registration and electoral systems, albeit on a smaller scale.

Before doing that, Lebanon prompts a pause to consider a subtle point from the Author's Note. The challenge to *"help us find a way through"* included reference to the "majority." But who constitute the majority? Simplistically, this might be obvious. A more nuanced approach than simply looking at ethnic and religious categorisations has been proposed by a Lebanese Christian.

Chapter 7

So who is the Majority?

We have noted the view, expressed by a Christian in the Middle East, that many Muslims appreciate religious registration because it identifies who belongs to the majority and hence should enjoy whatever benefits that brings. Who then is the majority?

We have already made one assertion that some Muslims would contest. We spoke of 'communities' – plural – when some would assert that there is one Muslim community. One theme in our tour is whether or not diversity within Islam is recognised, respected and embraced.

Lebanon formally recognises such diversity, allowing separate millets for Sunnis, Shi'a and others. But even in Lebanon they have one senior Mufti, leader – in some sense – of all Muslims. Lebanon is an exception to the more common pattern whereby most Middle Eastern countries treat all Muslims as part of the one millet. Most countries assert that they treat them all equally before the law; however in practice many differentiate and discriminate against those not of the same tradition as the rulers. In most cases, this means that the majority marginalises the minority, such as Egyptian Sunnis treating Egyptian Shi'a badly. However, Syria – which is at the end of our tour – is an exception because the President and many members of his inner circle come from a minority tradition – the Alawites – which, in some respects, marginalised the Sunni majority.

There are similar examples in the Arabian Peninsula where Saudi Arabia marginalises its Shi'a citizens (estimated as 10-15%) whilst in Bahrain the rulers are typically Sunni and repress the Shi'a despite there being approximately twice as many Shi'a as Sunnis.

The concept of who is the majority is therefore more nuanced than it may appear.

The use of a single millet for all Muslims enables cross-tradition marriages, with the couple trusted to negotiate how they live and in which tradition they will instruct their children. In chapter 18 we will discover a city where Sunni-Shi'a marriages were common until recent times.

Another theme is how one determines who is a Muslim. Religious registration can make this clear although it ignores factors such as how an individual lives or how a community conducts its affairs. What is the role of ethics, behaviour and attitudes, to say nothing of religious belief and practice? So does religious registration really identify who is a Muslim? Surely the answer is, only if one excludes belief, practice and lifestyle.

In recent years Syrian Christian leaders have asked an association of Western Christians not to refer to their communities as a 'minority.' They point out that no group forms a majority under an ethnic-religious-tribal view of society. Labelling them as a minority differentiates them from society as a whole, making them more vulnerable. Instead they request that Syria's Christian communities be described as an integral part of a multi-ethnic and multi-religious society. Segregating society on religious lines is not helpful.

Similarly, we noted that some members of Turkey's Christian communities had suggested that it is not helping them to think of themselves as minorities, since it tends to imply that they should be quiet for fear of attracting attention. A more positive and outward looking view is being prompted by some; a view that says Christians are an historic and integral part of society, whose presence enriches the whole.

So how might we determine who is a majority? In October 2014 an alternative approach was suggested by Dr. Martin Accad, who is Lebanese. He suggests that if one looks for those who desire the best for all fellow citizens, who seek to use their religious belief and practice as a motivation for seeking and serving the common good, then such people would be a clear majority.[7]

So, who the majority is depends on how one chooses to look. People of goodwill far outnumber those who choose violent and repressive methods. Across the Middle East, people who respect and value diversity and who regard diversity as an asset that enriches society as a whole far outnumber those who seek to impose uniformity.

[7] Martin Accad on the Institute of Middle East Studies Blog, 2nd October 2014;
https://imeslebanon.wordpress.com/2014/10/02/christians-at-the-heart-of-the-middle-easts-future/ (accessed 26th February 2015)

Chapter 8

Jordan – politics and millets

We began our tour of the region in Jordan, noting the intensity of some of the consequences for some individuals of the religious registration system. We return to consider how Jordan has adapted the Ottoman era system.

There is a diversity of Christian churches in Jordan. An estimated two to four percent of Jordanians have a religious registration of Christian. The percentage might be small but their presence is welcomed by senior government figures. During 2014, one commented that it is the Christians who hold the community together, both in Jordan and throughout the Middle East. He urged Christians not to emigrate. The message was repeated by King Abdullah on 24th September 2014 in an address to the UN General Assembly: "Let me say once again: Arab Christians are an integral part of my region's past, the present, and future."[8]

Personal status matters are handled exclusively within religion-based courts. Effectively there are four millets, one for Muslims and three for Christians.

The Muslim millet typically applies the Hanafi school of Islamic jurisprudence. Almost all Jordanian Muslims are Sunnis, with small numbers of Shi'a. There are also small Baha'i and Druze communities whose members come within this millet, although

---

[8] King Abdullah's English language website; 24th September 2014; http://kingabdullah.jo/index.php/en_US/speeches/view/id/546/videoDisplay/0.html (accessed 5th August 2015)

almost all Muslims regard the Baha'i faith as being outside of the family of Islam, as do most Baha'i.

The Muslim millet covers all citizens whose religious registration is Muslim. The minor children of a male who converts to Islam are automatically regarded as having also converted. However, at the age of 18 they may choose to revert to the registration they had at birth. If they do so, they will be ineligible to inherit from their father's estate. Jordan's Shari'a courts are operated under the Muslim millet. It was these courts that were used against Siham and Ramzi whose stories we read in chapter 1.

The three Christian millets are Greek Orthodox, Catholic and Anglican. Each millet has a tribunal, or Ecclesiastical Court, whose structure and members are determined by the respective churches. The Monarch's approval is required for judicial appointments within each tribunal. The government recognises the Council of Church Leaders as its advisory body for all Christian religious affairs. The Council comprises the heads of the country's 11 officially recognised Christian churches. Of these, one is Eastern Orthodox, two are Oriental Orthodox, three are Catholic, four are Protestant and one falls outside this categorisation, namely the Assyrian Church of the

East. Their members within Jordan must approach one of the Christian millets for their personal status legal matters. The same is true for all Christians, although for most the choice is straightforward; they choose the one from their own tradition.

This arrangement forces the Christian communities to work together. This is not always easy, and some Jordanian Christians lament the difficulties, misunderstandings and tensions that arise from different priorities amongst the churches. One source of such difficulties relates to how different churches interact with Jordan's Muslim communities. There are reasons why this is controversial, which we shall explore in chapter 17.

The Baptist church is registered as a denomination but does not enjoy the same privileges as the other 11 recognised denominations. The Baptist church and four other Protestant denominations have formed a joint council – the Evangelical Synod – and applied to the Royal Court for recognition as a denomination and the right to operate their own ecclesiastical court. These churches have long enjoyed legal status under a law of 1953. Amendments to the legislation governing ecclesiastical courts made during 2014 defined more clearly a mechanism to grant a church the right to operate an Ecclesiastical Court upon recommendation by the Minister of the Interior to the Prime Minister. These amendments did not include granting the Evangelical Synod the right to operate a court. It remains the case that a recommendation is unlikely to be made without support from the Council of Church Leaders.

Significantly, the amended Christian Communities Council Law provides that those churches that do not operate an Ecclesiastical Court will no longer be able to choose to be governed by the court of another church. Rather, personal status issues are to be handled by the Ordinary (First Instance) courts. This applies to the churches of the Evangelical Synod, together with others including Lutherans, Maronites, Chaldeans, Armenian and Syriac Catholics. These churches are concerned that the First Instance courts have no experience of dealing with Ecclesiastical issues, and some have objected that this would constitute unacceptable state intervention in fundamental issues of Christian sacrament, notably marriage. This concern arises from marriage being treated as a religious sacrament by some churches, putting it on a par with baptism and what is referred to as Mass, Eucharist, Communion or 'the Lord's supper' by different strands within Christianity.

No Christian traditions in Jordan make provision for divorce. Consequently, a Christian couple who desire to divorce are obliged to change their religious registration to Muslim, whereupon a divorce is easy to secure. We need to be aware that this has long-term consequences – those who take this option cannot revert to being registered as Christian.

Jordan, like most Middle Eastern countries, forbids Muslim women from marrying non-Muslims. In contrast, Muslim men may marry non-Muslim women, with the lady's registration being changed to Muslim as a direct consequence of her marriage. This system is resented by some Jordanian church leaders as it disadvantages their communities; their young ladies may leave but other Jordanians are not able to join. As one church leader articulated, what the Christian community desires is that such mixed-religion couples be allowed to decide for themselves which religious community they would be part of and which faith – or faiths – they would instruct their children in.

This imbalance in the religious registration system is one reason why the percentage of the population registered as Christian is declining. Other significant factors are higher emigration rates and lower birth rates amongst Christians when compared with Muslim communities. Similar factors affect the changing religious demographics in other countries in the Middle East.

We noted at the start of this chapter that the presence of Christians is deeply appreciated by Jordan's political elite. This is also demonstrated in the linkage of the religious registration system with the political system. The lower house of parliament, *The Chamber of Deputies*, is an elected body of 150 members. 108 Deputies are elected in single member constituencies and 27 are elected using a nationwide party list system. The remaining 15 seats are reserved for women, namely those with the most votes but not directly elected in the single member constituencies. The 108 directly elected seats include nine reserved for Christians and three for those of Chechen or Circassian origin. In practice, Christians may be candidates in any constituency subject to the usual nomination procedure but in nine seats non-Christians are not allowed to be candidates. The same applies for the three seats reserved for those of Chechen or Circassian origin. As with Turkey, some people were displaced into what is now Jordan due to conflict in the Circassian and other parts of the North Caucasus region during the nineteenth century.

The party list element was introduced in 2012 in a package of reforms that also increased the number of Deputies from 110 to 150. This package of measures only partially addressed one major concern with the previous system, namely that it was very uneven. In rural areas each Deputy typically represents 2,000-3,000 constituents compared with more than 90,000 per Deputy in the capital, Amman. Analysts suggested two reasons why this was maintained. First, to ensure more representatives of ethnically Jordanian origin (as distinct from those of Palestinian origin) than strict demographics would imply. Second, the late King Hussein had adjusted the distribution to disadvantage those provinces where Islamist parties had strong support. Consequently, the best known opposition party, the Islamic Action Front, boycotted the parliamentary election held on 23rd January 2013 because it claimed that the electoral system continued to be biased in favour of certain communities.

The government continues to retain control over political developments. Its affirmation of the presence of Christians is welcome although it is abundantly clear that this welcome does not extend to those whose religious registration is Muslim who choose to become Christians. In chapter 1 we saw two examples of such people feeling compelled to leave the country.

We will return to electoral systems in chapter 10 when we consider some aspects of the Arab Awakening.

One other aspect of the relationship between the government and Christians is worth exploring. Typically, the government discourages Christians from working in the public sector. Whether this is official policy or simply the actions of officials is debateable. Jordan's Palestinian citizens face similar discrimination. The consequence is that Christians are forced to seek employment in the private sector and to be entrepreneurial. It is of note that Christians own a disproportionately high percentage of businesses and commercial operations. This makes them valuable citizens and contributors to society.

As we conclude our time in Jordan let us reflect on how many people are directly affected by the challenges that religious registration creates. The whole of the recognised Christian community is affected by the challenges described in this chapter.

The case studies we examined in chapter 1 illustrate what can happen to some individuals. There are numerous stories of those who choose to become Christians being assaulted by family members, as Ramzi was, or being threatened. Some choose to leave Jordan. Some are harassed by the authorities. Such cases are not made public for fear of aggravating the situation. Many are aware that Shari'a courts can act in draconian ways against converts. The challenges of religious registration are widely felt.

For now, our journey will take us to a second visit to Egypt, a country with a long history and an equally long river. It is a country where mixed religious registration marriages have proven problematic for some. Like Jordan, the Christian community owns and operates a disproportionately high percentage of the privately-owned businesses.

Chapter 9

Egypt – glorious past, what of the future?

I enjoy visiting Egypt. It has a vibrancy as well as a long and distinguished history. The pyramids at Giza are the only one of the seven wonders of the ancient world to remain standing. Another of those ancient wonders was the lighthouse of Alexandria, which now lies in ruins on the seabed. Alexandria was where the Hebrew scriptures were translated into Greek, evidence that it once had a thriving Jewish community.

I think of Egypt as having two major waterways. The river Nile pushes its blue ribbon way of life through what would otherwise be desert. Driving east from Cairo I saw a ship's bridge and cargo of containers, evidence that we were approaching the Suez Canal. The pyramids were built as magnificent tombs for the dead. What, I always wonder, is the place of the living? Egypt has a rich past, it remains at a crossroads of world trade. What about its people today? One theme of this chapter is the effects of religious registration on the vibrancy of modern day Egypt.

For me, Cairo airport is a place of welcome and safe transit between air and ground transportation systems. In contrast, the airport has proven to be a dangerous place for some Egyptians whose religious registration is Muslim but who have chosen to become Christians. As we saw in chapter 2, such people cannot change their registration if they were registered as Muslim at birth. In this chapter we look at some of the challenges they face, especially for women, concerning whom the state will allow them to marry.

On 13th December 2008, Martha was arrested at Cairo airport. On 16th December she was charged with falsifying official documents and was remanded in custody for 15 days. Why? Martha became a Christian in 2003 but her religious registration remained as Muslim. She acquired false documents enabling her to adopt a Christian name and obtain an identity card stating that she was a Christian. An Egyptian woman whose religious registration is Muslim is only allowed to marry a man whose registration is likewise Muslim. The acquired documents enabled her to marry a Christian man which she duly did. The couple have two children, born in 2004 and 2006. They were aware of the risks should the change of identity be discovered and so they decided to leave Egypt. They were at Cairo airport en-route to a new life in another country when Martha was arrested. Earlier in our tour we encountered people who chose to relocate because of persecution. In Martha's case, it was in attempting to relocate that her family's problems began.

Martha's husband and children were also arrested but released after a few days. The husband was re-arrested but released nine days later when Martha stated in court that he did not know about the false documents. Martha was released without charge in February 2009, two months after her arrest at Cairo airport. All the family's legal documents had been seized and a freeze placed on their receiving new documents which prevented the family from leaving Egypt. The family began to live in hiding for fear that Martha's relatives would seek custody of the children. We have noted this in the cases of Siham, Ramzi and Muna.

On 10th December 2010 Martha and her husband were summoned to a court hearing on criminal charges of identity theft. They remained in hiding. Both husband and wife received 15 year sentences in absentia. A further consequence of this ruling is that the couple's marriage is not recognised by the state and the children are 'wards of the State,' thus denying the parents legal custody of their children. The family continued living in hiding. The religious registration issue has denied them the legitimacy of their marriage, the custody in law of their children and forced them to live in hiding.

A similar incident occurred in 2009. A single female convert from Islam to Christianity was arrested at Cairo airport and sentenced to one year's hard labour for identity theft, having obtained, but not used, an identity card stating she was Christian. She served nine months of the sentence. When released she was placed under de-facto house arrest by her family. In 2011 her family started permitting her to leave the home.

Since 2010 the government has improved its information technology systems, primarily motivated by the desire to reduce benefit fraud. One side-effect is that more cases are being discovered where people with a religious registration of Muslim have acquired documents stating that they are Christians. For example, in January 2013 a lady and her seven children were each sentenced to 15 years' imprisonment for changing their identity documents to use Christian names. The lady converted to Islam when she married a Muslim. When he died in 1991 she reverted to being a Christian and encouraged her children to convert. In 2004 each family member obtained new, fraudulent, documents using Christian names and the family moved town. In 2006 one of the sons was arrested on suspicion of having forged identity papers. He confessed to the police, citing his mother as the instigator. Seven civil servants were also convicted and sentenced to five years' imprisonment for their role in providing false documents.

We should note that those who use illegal methods usually encounter problems as a result at some point. We acknowledge that desperate people sometimes choose to do desperate things and there are all too many situations where there are seemingly no good options. I cannot condone illegal and fraudulent methods within the identity card system, neither will I condemn those whose options to act as law-abiding citizens are severely restricted. Legal systems that provide some citizens with no good, lawful options should be carefully examined and reformed.

We noted in chapter 6 that in Lebanon people with different religious registrations can marry abroad and the marriage is recognised and accepted by the state.

This is not the case in Egypt. Should an Egyptian woman whose religious registration is Muslim marry abroad a man whose registration is Christian, then the Egyptian government refuses to recognise the marriage. Further, the authorities are alerted to the lady's choice of religion, which can lead to discrimination. Officials have been known to refuse to process a passport renewal application for a lady they knew had converted to Christianity.

Regarding marriage, there are some Egyptians who are unable to register their marriage with the state authorities. Religious registration in Egypt is limited to 'Muslim, Christian, Jew and —', with the latter applied to the Baha'i. There are religiously-based court systems for Muslims, Christians and Jews, but not for the Baha'i. There is also a civil system, primarily for expatriates, to which nationals have no access. The Baha'i can marry within their faith but there is no mechanism by which the state recognises the marriage.

One long-running situation that continues in Egypt concerns Wafaa Constantine. This case started in December 2004 when she left her home following a marital dispute. Some Muslims claimed that Wafaa had converted to Islam. This prompted a large protest from the church and Christians who claimed that Wafaa had been kidnapped by Muslims. The political authorities responded by collecting Wafaa from the place where she was residing, taking her to a monastery and handing her over to the church. According to the church, she had not converted to Islam and wanted to remain a Christian.

In October 2008 there were unsubstantiated rumours that Wafaa had been killed. In 2013 a lawsuit was issued demanding that the authorities either published a death certificate or disclosed her location. In January 2014 an administrative court postponed a hearing until 5th March 2014. There have been no reports of any further developments. We must conclude that either those submitting the case quietly withdrew it or that the authorities have decided to do nothing rather than risk mob violence in response to whatever judgement the court might make.

Underlying Wafaa's situation is the question of who is entitled to say that someone has converted and, if so, whether this is recognised by the authorities as expressed in their religious registration. In this case, the one person whose views are not being heard expressed in person in public is the person at the centre of the story. Wafaa appears to have become a pawn in a game played by others.

In recent years there have been numerous reports of Christian girls being coerced to convert to Islam. Some claim that the victims are kidnapped and forcibly married in order to make them part of the Muslim community. The reports do not always reflect the whole truth, as in some situations the young lady has either genuinely fallen in love or wishes to leave the family for personal reasons. In such cases, their families are ashamed to reveal the truth. In contrast, there are known cases of attempts to trick Christian girls into compromising situations with a view to forcing their conversion to Islam. Some cases do involve girls who are minors. It is rarely possible for anyone to obtain interviews with all those involved in any particular situation, making a verifiable statement of the facts impossible to obtain.

Situations in which Christian girls have converted to Islam are often controversial, with it being difficult to verify claims of it being their considered choice, the result of coercion or overt force proving impossible to verify. For our purposes here, being sure of who has 'converted' to what can be obscured, just as it is for Wafaa. We will return to the subject of forced or coerced conversion, and the recognition or otherwise of such, in chapter 18.

Egypt retains a central role in the unfolding developments that were first labelled as 'The Arab Spring' which we will explore in the next chapter. Suffice to say here that in Tahrir Square, Independence Square, the placards of 2011 stated that *"We are citizens, we are all one."* This is not yet the case regarding restrictions on marriage.

There are other challenges to the calls that all Egyptians be treated equally; inter-communal harmony has been known to break down on occasions in parts of the country. Such issues affect individuals, communities and property. A common local response is to hold a *reconciliation meeting* involving those involved in the incident, normally with the assistance of local community leaders. Such meetings have no official standing in law and therefore neither fulfil nor remove the State's legal obligation to file cases against perpetrators of assaults and threats where there is clear evidence that a criminal act has been committed. In many cases *reconciliation meetings* result in members of minorities being forced to accept a degree of injustice and allow perpetrators to escape legal sanction for their crimes. Two examples illustrate this.

On 20th March 2011 Ayman Anwar Mitri was attacked in Qena over an alleged affair. His ear was cut off. Ayman is a Christian and his attacker a Muslim. On 23rd March a *reconciliation meeting* was held at which one assailant acknowledged that the accusation was false and apologised for the unwarranted assault. In this case the police did proceed with a case against the attackers. On 22nd April 2012 a judge exonerated and released the attackers following intense pressure on Ayman to pardon them.

On 28th January 2012 a large mob of Muslims attacked Christian owned homes and businesses in Kobry-el-Sharbat (el-Ameriyah), Alexandria Province. Two Christians and one Muslim were injured. A rumour had circulated that a Christian man had an intimate photo of a Muslim woman on his mobile phone. Violence erupted and a number of *reconciliation meetings* between Muslim and Christian leaders were held. Initially, Muslim leaders were insistent that all Christian families must leave the village. Eight families were forced to leave, with the sale of their homes and businesses overseen by a Muslim leader. On 16th February a parliamentary fact-finding commission issued a proclamation cancelling all evictions and confiscations of property, and asserting that the law gave all Christian families the right to reside in the village. The commission included two Christians, two moderate Muslims and a Salafist (see Glossary) MP who had been involved in the *reconciliation meetings*. In this case, the parliamentary commission overturned at least some of the injustice that the *reconciliation meeting* had imposed. Nothing was done about the perpetrators of criminal acts of vandalism.

What is understood by *reconciliation* in situations like these? In practice it means that there will be harmony if the minority community agrees to live with whatever conditions the majority stipulates. Right and wrong, in the sense of what is lawful and criminal, is a secondary consideration. It is establishing peace in the sense of an end to overt conflict, effectively by the unconditional surrender of the weaker party. It is not peace and harmony in the sense of a mutual respect that recognises and affirms distinctions and differences and seeks to allow everyone to flourish.

In sectarian incidents involving Muslims and Christians we need to keep in mind that it is the religious registration system that underpins the treatment of Christians as a minority and consequently as powerless and obliged to be *reconciled* in the sense of accepting whatever the majority imposes. If the thinking became that people of goodwill are the majority as discussed in chapter 7 then perhaps criminal behaviour would be treated for what it is, irrespective of the registration of the perpetrators and victims.

Another area in which Christians and Muslims are treated differently in Egypt has emerged since 2011. Egypt's blasphemy laws date from the President Mubarak era (i.e. 1981-2011) but were applied very rarely. This changed in 2012 when at least three Christians were imprisoned after being convicted on blasphemy charges. All denied any wrongdoing and noted that due attention was not paid to the evidence during their trials. A higher profile case started on 9th May 2013 when Demiana, a 24-year old Christian teacher, was arrested following complaints by a number of parents and pupils concerning the content of a class she taught on 8th April 2013. Two independent investigations were conducted, one by the school council representing parents and teachers and the other by the local office of the Ministry of Education. Both found no basis for the allegations. Ten of the thirteen pupils interviewed during these investigations stated that the accusations were false.

Despite this, lawyers representing the parents of one pupil went to the prosecutor's office and filed a complaint. This prompted the arrest and a court case. Demiana was released on bail before the end of May. On 11th June she was convicted. The judge did not give her a custodial sentence but imposed a fine of EGP 100,000 (approximately US$14,000). An appeal was submitted. In February 2014 the defence lawyer reported that the judge had agreed that the report of an investigation in May 2013 could be read to a court during an appeal hearing. The report exonerated Demiana. She was cleared on appeal but denied permission to return to her job. Demiana consistently denied any wrongdoing. Fearing a custodial sentence, she went into hiding shortly before the 11th June hearing. Her life was irreversibly changed by the false accusations and the failure to apply the law justly.

In Egypt's honour-shame culture, right and wrong, legal and illegal is of less significance than what is perceived to be honourable and shameful. We need to ask what in Demiana's situation is honourable about the conduct of those who falsely accused her and sat in judgement of her. Is it truly honourable to ignore evidence and the outcomes of independent investigations? Is it truly honourable to effectively end the career of a young teacher to satisfy the whims of a few?

One factor in much injustice is poor police procedures, or poor application of such procedures, in handling complaints and initial investigations. An extreme example of this occurred in al-Kosheh in 1998 concerning the murder of two Christians. The events that followed and the intertwined web of social, economic, political and religious factors involved are documented by Charles Sennott in his book *The Body and the Blood*.[9] In summary, numerous Christian residents of the area were detained and brutally interrogated whilst the police chose not to investigate suspects who had religious registration of Muslim. The injustice in this first criminal act created tensions that erupted in sectarian violence on 31st December 1999.

The religious registration system in Egypt affects numerous areas of society. Muslims who choose to become Christians are forced to live with the challenges of their identity card stating a religious registration which is different from their religious

[9] Charles Sennott; *The Body and the Blood* (paperback edition); (Public Affairs, 2013) chapter VII, especially pages 167-173 and 191.

belief. Some such people have no good options for marrying the person they love. Collectively, the honourable resolution of sectarian clashes is compromised by the overt identification of the religious communities to which participants belong. This is contrary to the origins of religious registration which were to affirm distinct religious communities as loyal to the political rulers whilst conducting personal status matters according to their own customs. All those whose religious registration is not Muslim are at risk of becoming victims of such injustices, as also are Muslims known not to be Sunnis.

Since 2011 additional aspirations, expectations and opportunities have been released within Egyptian society, notably the call that all Egyptians are citizens. This prompts us to pause in our regional tour to look at this topic in the next chapter. I prefer to call it the "Arab Awakening."

Chapter 10

The Arab Awakening – a changing context

Our purpose in this chapter is to highlight that the context has changed, is changing, and will continue to change in the Middle East. We then ask what the possible ramifications are for the religious registration systems currently in place across the Middle East. The intention here is not to provide a comprehensive review, which would be a book in itself.

It is worth remembering the original calls of the protesters in 2011. Common themes were a call for an end to corruption and nepotism, for an end to state brutality, for better job prospects and for a voice in the country's governance. In summary, a scream for dignity for all. The details varied from country to country and we need to be aware that every Arab country has been affected to a greater or lesser degree.

Several countries have sought to quietly revise their governance structures. Both the rulers and the majority of the population seek a gradual, evolutionary process; they are keen to avoid a revolution. Morocco, Oman and Jordan are the clearest examples. There have been constitutional amendments and changes to election systems, as in Jordan (chapter 8).

Amidst everything, one image stands out for me. Egyptians in Tahrir Square, Cairo, held up placards stating *"We are citizens, we are all one."* Muslims and Christians joined together in such calls. At one point Muslims protected Christians as they prayed and then the Christians stood around Muslims to enable them to pray in safety.

What was originally referred to as "The Arab Spring" is commonly dated to the beginning of 2011. One trigger point occurred on 17th December 2010 when Mohamed Bouazizi self-immolated in Sidi Bouzid, a small town in Tunisia. He had been prevented from trying to earn a modest living by selling vegetables from an informal, mobile stand. The authorities confiscated his stand and produce, ostensibly because he did not have a licence. When he politely requested that his goods be returned the authorities sent him away empty handed. The next they knew was his act of utter desperation. As we noted in the previous chapter, desperate people sometimes resort to desperate means. This act of a man setting fire to himself because he was unable to earn a living sparked widespread protests in Tunisia leading to long-standing President Ben Ali leaving office and the country on 14th January 2011. Mohamed Bouazizi, a desperate man, had set fire to much more than a small amount of fuel poured over his body.

Popular protests in Egypt led to the removal from office of President Mubarak on 11th February 2011. This led to a period of military rule during which the constitution was revised and parliamentary and presidential elections held. On 30th June 2012 Mohammed Morsi was sworn into office as President of Egypt. Later in 2012 the constitution was revised again. The constitutional court ruled part of the parliamentary election process unconstitutional thereby dissolving the lower house of parliament. In April 2013 widespread discontent emerged about President Morsi's governance and on 3rd July the military removed him from office. A revision of the constitution was approved by a national referendum in January 2014. This was the third such revision in three years.

It is no longer possible for anyone to govern Egypt against the will of public opinion. In 2011 and again in

2013 people were willing to continue protesting even when violence was used against them. The system of governance might be little changed and few of the original calls of protesters have been met. Yet, the culture within the country has changed. As one Egyptian put it to me in June 2013, "In the long term, ten to fifteen years, I am very optimistic; better rights for all will be established. However, I am very nervous about the near term; it is not clear how peaceful the transition will be."

July and August 2013 were not peaceful in Egypt, with loss of life and property damage affecting many Egyptians, including Christians as numerous church buildings were damaged by rioters. Let us note the optimism for the future. What are the implications for Egypt's religious registration system of the calls for all to be citizens and for the establishment of better rights for all? Do young Egyptians embrace a system that restricts who can marry whom? I think not.

A number of people in the Middle East have pointed out that several events which occurred prior to 2011 proved significant in setting the context for the Arab Spring. In Lebanon in March 2005 there was a mass protest involving one million people, approximately a quarter of the population, against the continuing overt

Syrian presence in Lebanon. The protest followed the assassination of Prime Minister Rafik Hariri on 14th February 2005 and it led to the withdrawal of Syria's official military and security presence. None of the protests of 2011 involved even close to a quarter of the population. However, the June 2013 protests in Egypt that led to the removal of President Morsi involved at least a third of the population.

In Egypt, three events are cited as contributing to the motivation of protesters. First, in June 2010 Khaled Said died in custody in Alexandria. There was widespread condemnation on social media within Egypt, which led to the prosecution of several police officers. This was the first time in living memory that members of the security services had been held to account for brutality against detainees. Further, a parliamentary election held in November 2010 was regarded as so well stage-managed by President Mubarak's ruling party that almost all opposition parties boycotted the poll. The electoral process was widely regarded as a sham. Finally, on 1st January 2011, 21 Christians were killed in a bomb attack at a church building in Alexandria. Many Muslims as well as Christians were appalled. There were suggestions that members of the Interior Ministry were implicated in the crime. The official explanation blamed militants based in the Gaza Strip, although some saw this as an example of blaming outsiders rather than confronting the actual local reality.

The term "Arab Spring" is no longer helpful. The use of a single phrase implies a uniformity when the reality is a great diversity. The means, objectives and results of protests are widely different across the region. Further, the use of the word "Spring" implies a positive and hopeful process, as well as a linear progression. As events became more violent in more places, this word could no longer be seen as appropriate.

The use of the word "Arab" is also problematic as it ignores the numerous ethnic groups within the Middle East and North Africa who do not regard themselves as "Arabs." Examples include the Kurds in Iran, Iraq, Syria and Turkey and the various Berber groups across North Africa.

As a brief aside, I find the term "Arab world" increasingly unhelpful. It is typically a Western construct that over-simplifies the diversity amongst the many states, the majority of whose populations are ethnically Arab. It is also worth noting that labels can be problematic whilst also being revealing. In chapter 8 we noted Jordan's King Abdullah use of the term "Arab Christians." Others use the term "Christian Arabs." Linguistically, which is the noun and which the adjective? Are we referring to people who are Arab and happen to be Christian or are we describing people who are Christian and happen to be Arab? I have heard Christians in the Middle East use both in different contexts. King Abdullah used the former, identifying with his subjects who are of a different religion to himself.

I have heard some Christians in the Middle East trying to distance themselves from being identified as "Arabs"; some Egyptian Christians describe themselves as ethnically Pharaonic, some Lebanese Christians describe themselves as ethnically Phoenician and many Iraqi Christians describe themselves as Chaldo-Assyrians.

We can note the existence of the Arab League, a multinational organisation with 22 members. Somalia is one of several members whose population are not ethnically Arab and where Arabic is rarely used. The term Arab is used in this context in a broad sense.

So a new term for the Arab Spring needed to emerge, with different titles being used by some. All retained use of the word Arab, despite the concerns expressed by some. Jeremy Bowen entitled his 2012 book *The Arab Uprisings – the People Demand the Fall of the Regime*. This fits well with his focus on Egypt, Libya, Syria and Tunisia but excludes the effects felt in other countries. Of note is his observation that, historically, most revolutions are messy and many ultimately end with similar governance to that which the instigators set out to replace. Superficially, this is the case in Egypt but, as we noted earlier in this chapter, the underlying culture has changed and optimism for the longer term remains. We will see later that Bowen's assessment appears to be true in one country in the Middle East that had a revolution in 1979.

The term "Arab Awakening" is used in the title of a book by Marwan Muasher, a former Foreign Minister and Deputy Prime Minister of Jordan. His title is *The Second Arab Awakening and the Battle for Pluralism*. Muasher treats the Arab's revolt against the Ottomans before and during World War One as the first Arab Awakening. The outcome of this awakening was that "colonial autocracies were replaced by domestic ones – often military backed single parties that took advantage of their revolutionary legitimacy to cement their grip on power."[10] The author notes that human society cannot thrive and flourish without pluralism. He argues that "only when societies and their elected leaders truly embrace tolerance, diversity, the peaceful rotation of power and inclusive economic growth can the promise of a new Arab world be realised."[11]

Muasher confronts the concept of patronage that is prevalent within many Middle Eastern cultures. Patronage assumes that there are limited resources and few opportunities for individuals and groups. Therefore, people seek a champion or provider, i.e. a patron, who will provide them with resources and opportunities in return for loyalty. In many cases, people seek to imitate their patron. Typically, people look to their father or tribal elder as their patron; some look to their government; others to non-state actors including armed groups.

Musasher notes that:

---

[10] Marwan Muasher; *The Second Arab Awakening and the Battle for Pluralism*; (Yale University Press, 2014) page 1
[11] Ibid; page 4

"the Arab world will go through a period of turmoil in which exclusionist forces will attempt to dominate the landscape with absolute truths and new dictatorships. These forces will also fade, because in the end, the exclusionist, authoritarian discourses cannot answer the people's need for a better quality of life – economically, politically, culturally and otherwise. As history has demonstrated overwhelmingly, where there is respect for diversity, there is prosperity. Contrary to what Arab societies have been taught for decades by their governments to believe – that tolerance, acceptance of different points of view, and critical thinking are destructive to national unity and economic growth – experience proves that societies cannot keep renewing themselves and thereby thrive except through diversity. Neither the theological model of Wilayat-al-Faqih nor the secular, authoritarian model of the Mubarak regime has succeeded in solving the region's economic, political, or cultural challenges."[12]

The literal meaning of Wilayat-al-Faqih is 'Guardianship of the Jurist.' It is the theological basis within Shi'a Islam adopted by Ayatollah Ruhollah Khomeini to justify the constitution adopted by Iran following its 1979 revolution. We shall explore this further in chapter 12.

One aspect of the Arab Awakening that we need to acknowledge is the violence that has occurred. In some countries violence has been limited to protestors versus police and other security services at some protests. Elsewhere it has sparked widespread use of military conflict involving government controlled armed forces and numerous armed groups. The events of 2011 have led to violent conflicts in Libya and Syria in particular, and have exacerbated conflict in parts of Egypt, Iraq, Lebanon, Sudan and Yemen.

Many armed groups are formed on tribal lines as part of each tribe's desire to protect themselves and their property, and ensure some stability for their

[12] Ibid; pages 184-5

community. This is the case in much of Libya and Yemen, and also for the Kurdish communities in Syria. Other armed groups are formed around an ideology, some secular and progressive and others (including most of the well known ones) based on various interpretations of Islam. The most notorious is the one that renamed itself "The Islamic State" in June 2014 after taking control of parts of Iraq to add to those parts of Syria where it exercised administrative control. This group's brutality has become notorious. In Syria their view was to forcibly displace Christians to Beirut whilst adherents of Shi'a Islam were to be killed. We will discuss this group further in chapters 13 and 18. For now we note that it is, to use Muasher's phrase, an exclusionist force, and one that treats Muslims of other traditions in even more extreme ways that it does adherents of other faiths.

I trust that Muasher will be seen to be correct; that exclusionist forces, some of which use violent means, will fade, even disappear, from the Middle East. At present, this appears unlikely to be a quick process.

There are examples of political leaders seeking to address the challenge of exclusionist forces. One we will see in chapter 22. In Egypt, we can note two actions by President Sisi. On 1st January 2015 in a speech at al-Azhar University – the foremost academic institution in Sunni Islam – he asked that they lead an examination of sacred texts to counter extremist ideology within Islam.[13] (Appendix 4 notes that Al-Azhar was involved in reformist movements within Islam in the early decades of the twentieth century.) Five days later he attended a Christmas Eve service in St. Mark's Cathedral in central Cairo, the first time an Egyptian president has ever attended such an event.[14] His attendance was welcomed by Christians as a significant recognition of their place within Egyptian society. It is also an overt challenge to the exclusionist view of some Muslims that it is wrong to greet adherents of other faiths as they celebrate their religious festivals. It is a small step in addressing the pluralism deficit.

I find that even in the West, pluralism is not always properly understood. I think of pluralism in two ways. First, in a corporate and somewhat passive way as being about the expectation that people of different

---

[13] See for example The Cairo Post; 2nd January 2015; http://www.thecairopost.com/news/132144/news/al-azhar-responds-to-sisis-call-for-religious-revolution; accessed 19th February 2015

[14] In the Eastern tradition of Christianity, Christmas is celebrated on 7th January, as opposed to 25th December in the Western tradition.

social classes, religions, ethnicities, nationalities, etc. are able to co-exist together in a harmonious society. Second, in a personal and active way as the need to intentionally seek to see other people's points of view as a demonstration of one's belief in the validity of a diversity of views and practices.

The former views pluralism as something that needs to be accepted but contains little imperative for how each individual is expected to behave. The latter states that being pluralistic is about an attitude that affects behaviour; it looks for and welcomes alternative views; it celebrates diversity.

Muasher's book might be summarised as a plea for the pluralism deficit to be addressed:

> "The Arab world will miss a golden opportunity if it does not give diversity and pluralism the attention they deserve. A new culture needs to be nurtured. No individual or party can claim monopoly on the truth

and still expect a prosperous society to emerge."[15]

He argues that greater respect for diversity within societies across the Middle East would improve the economic vibrancy of the region, which is an essential requirement to meeting the calls for more and better jobs, because it would facilitate foreign investment.[16]

In Lebanon (chapter 6) we noted that one of the newly appointed Mufti's first acts was to speak of the need for an end to Sunni-Shi'a tensions; in other words, for greater pluralism within Islam and amongst Muslim communities.

The region is being profoundly shaken and shaped by socio-political-economic changes in the world. Satellite TV and, more recently, the internet have made many aware of the relative state of the Middle East compared to other regions of the world. Many young people in the Middle East are asking why their societies are not doing better. Social media allows new means of expression and new ways to organise. Rising populations lead to greater pressures on

[15] Marwan Muasher; *The Second Arab Awakening and the Battle for Pluralism*; (Yale University Press, 2014) page 27
[16] Ibid; page 173, "Holistic Reform"

education systems and create the need for more employment opportunities. Urbanisation is drawing ever more people to the region's cities and major towns; Cairo and Istanbul in particular are amongst the world's mega-cities. Generational differences are increasingly prevalent, notably in dress codes, methods of communication and greater individualism. The region's rich and diverse history suggests that it can thrive in global terms once more. Many of those who participated in protests are seeking effective leadership that governs for the benefit of all, not the preservation of the privileges of the few. This applies nationally and locally, as well as politically, economically and socially. Social change will, at some point, lead to changes in legal frameworks, including that underpinning religious registration.

We will pick up on these themes in chapter 28 when we ask in what ways religious registration affects the region; in what ways does it enable society to flourish and how does it limit, restrict or constrain society. To use a religious metaphor, in what ways is it a blessing and in what ways a curse? But we need to resume our tour; so let us move upstream along the River Nile from Egypt to Sudan.

Chapter 11

Sudan – a land of contrasts and conflicts

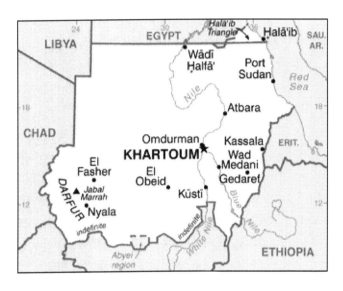

From Egypt, we move south upstream on the River Nile to Sudan, whose capital, Khartoum, is where the Blue Nile and White Nile meet. The source of the White Nile is Lake Victoria and the Mountains of the Moon in central Africa provide the steady, consistent year round supply of water that powers the Nile across the deserts of Sudan and Egypt. The Blue Nile rising in Ethiopia is more turbulent, with huge seasonal variation in river levels being the source of the annual flooding of the Nile that ancient Egypt depended on for its fertility. The presence of dams, first at Aswan in Egypt and now also in Sudan (and under construction in Ethiopia) control this abundant flow. Those areas near the rivers are fertile wheras much of the rest of Sudan is desert.

The Nile might be controlled but what about Sudan's diverse multi-ethnic peoples? Arabic might be the official language but numerous indigenous tribal languages remain in daily use. This is a country where no ethnic-religious group is close to being a majority. It is also a country that has seen much inter-tribal strife. Since the modern state was founded in 1956, there has been violent conflict in most parts for some of the time, and in some areas for most of the time.

Sudan changed on 9th July 2011 when South Sudan ceded from Sudan. Five days later South Sudan was unanimously accepted as a member of the United Nations.

Christians, in the religious registration sense, were deeply affected. Prior to the cessation of South Sudan, Sudan's population was estimated to be twenty percent Christian. Many either lived in what became South Sudan or in areas of Sudan close to the border with South Sudan, or were in the Khartoum area but of South Sudanese origin. Christian communities were disproportionately affected by what happened to those of South Sudanese origin. One immediate action in July 2011 was that the government of Sudan fired all government employees with South Sudanese origins. This profoundly affected the quality of government services, with consequences for the whole of society – an example of where exacerbating the pluralism deficit had adverse consequences for everyone.

One issue affecting many was whether they would be regarded as citizens of Sudan or the new state of South Sudan. South Sudan stated that it would grant citizenship to anyone living in Sudan who had at least one grandparent of South Sudanese origin. Of note here is that many people, all of whose grandparents originated in South Sudan, had never lived there themselves. Their parents or grandparents had migrated north to avoid civil conflict that has plagued many areas since independence in 1956. The separation failed to resolve the prevalence of inter-tribal strife; arguably the situation has worsened as further fault lines have appeared at ever more localised levels. The pluralism deficit is having a profound effect across Sudan.

The government of Sudan amended its citizenship law so that from 1st March 2012 onwards citizens would automatically lose their Sudanese citizenship when they acquired "de jure or de facto" the "nationality of South Sudan;" dual citizenship was not allowed. This law required those of South Sudanese origin to either leave or obtain work permits as expatriates in order to remain. Approximately half a million people were affected.

On 27th September 2012 Sudan and South Sudan signed an agreement on how to move forward on the question of citizenship rights for Southerners living in Sudan and Sudanese living in South Sudan. The two governments agreed to establish a Joint High Level Committee, led by their respective Ministries of Interior and incorporating other appropriate government officials, to negotiate the status and treatment of nationals in each country. A fine agreement on paper. Alas, by mid-2014, due to deterioration in the diplomatic relationship, there had been no progress on implementing it.

The practical effect of this is that the Sudanese government is able to assert that particular individuals are no longer citizens and can therefore be forced to leave. This continues to be applied to those registered as Christian.

Many of those who left Sudan experienced difficulties in transporting their possessions or moving their financial assets. Travel was either difficult or expensive, or both, as there were very few direct flights between Khartoum and Juba (the two capitals) and insecurity and border closures affected travel by road. Bureaucratic problems increased during 2012 and persisted throughout 2013 and 2014, a situation not helped by civil servants in Khartoum going unpaid due to the poor state of the government's finances.

In May 2014 religious registration issues in Sudan hit the headlines when Meriam Yahia Ibrahim Ishag was sentenced to death by hanging for apostasy. She had been arrested on 17th February 2014 and charged on 4th March with adultery and apostasy. Why?

Meriam claimed that she was raised as a Christian by her mother after her father left the home when she was six. To her, Christianity was the faith she was taught throughout her childhood and the one she adopted as her own. She met and married Daniel in Sudan. Daniel is of South Sudanese origin and also holds US citizenship. Like Meriam, he had been raised as a Christian and took his faith seriously.

The Sudanese government took a different view. Daniel, they accepted as a Christian in the religious registration sense, however, they stated that Meriam's father was registered as a Muslim and therefore Meriam too must have a registration of Muslim. Consequently, if she identified herself as a Christian she must have committed apostasy. Further, her marriage to a man registered as a Christian was illegal and therefore null and void. Because she had a son, born in September 2012, and was pregnant, she was evidently guilty of adultery. The authorities put the son in prison with his mother because they regarded him as a Muslim and would not allow him to be raised by his father, a Christian. The son's registration was following his mother's because she was being regarded as a single mother and, as we noted with Siham in Jordan, children registered as Muslims must be raised by those with Muslim registration.

Meriam appeared in court on 11th May where she was convicted of apostasy for which the Sudanese Penal Code mandates the death sentence. She was given three days to recant and informed that if she refused to revert to Islam then the sentence would be confirmed. At a court hearing on 15th May Meriam calmly confirmed to the judge that she was and would remain a Christian. The judge accordingly confirmed the sentence for apostasy of death by hanging. He also sentenced her to 100 lashes for adultery. The death sentence was to be imposed two years after she had given birth to their second child. An appeal was submitted.

One major legal complication was the disputed claims about Meriam's parents' identity and relevant details of her childhood, notably her schooling. In Sudan, religious education within the state school system follows the registration of each pupil, namely Islamic classes for Muslims and Christianity classes for Christians. So Meriam's school record would show what religious registration the authorities had recognised Meriam as having at that stage in her life. Such records were not made available to the court. One can surmise that if they had been found then they did not support the government's contention.

On 27th May Meriam gave birth to a daughter in the prison's clinic. The two year countdown to her execution began. On 23rd June an Appeal Court quashed the verdict and sentence. Meriam was released, together with her two young children.

In this case religious registration led to the imprisonment of a lady and her son, and to her second child being born in prison. She was convicted and sentenced despite serious disputes about the evidence; the Appeal Court's decision was based on procedural grounds, not factual matters. Sadly, Meriam's troubles, and those of her family, did not end when the appeal court quashed the conviction and sentence.

Some Sudanese citizens had called for her to be killed immediately. If she were released, they had said, then she should be murdered by a mob. This is neither the first nor last time on our regional tour that we will encounter the threat or actuality of mob violence. We noted in the previous chapter the underlying cause of a lack of respect and embracing of diversity: the pluralism deficit.

Taking such threats seriously, Meriam, together with Daniel, their young son and new born daughter, decided to leave Sudan. They were, however, arrested at Khartoum airport on 24th June by the Sudanese National Intelligence and Security Service. Meriam was accused of travelling using false documents. The family were released on bail the next day and taken into the care of the US Embassy in Khartoum, who had undertaken that the family would remain in Sudan pending the outcome of the authority's investigations. The travel documents had been issued by the Embassy of South Sudan, who attested that they were valid. Meriam's husband is of South Sudanese origin, which gives him entitlement to South Sudanese citizenship if he so chose. He also holds US citizenship, hence the involvement of the US Embassy.

On 24th July 2014 the Sudanese authorities allowed the family to leave Sudan and they flew to Rome on an Italian government aircraft. After a week in Italy, the family flew to the USA, where they moved to live near some of Daniel's relatives. They had relocated to somewhere that they had permanent residency. The challenges of becoming established, settled and self-supporting remain. Relocation is rarely simple.

What prompted the government to act against Meriam and her family in this manner? One suggestion is that the case was provoked by two men claiming to be her father and brother whose real motivation was to gain control of Daniel's thriving business. In court, Meriam stated that she did not recognise either claimant and the 'brother' failed to provide adequate answers when questioned about Meriam's schooling. Religious registration was applied in the case; there are numerous factors in the motivations of the various people involved including money, jealousy and religion.

In July 2014 the Sudan Council of Churches described the legal situation of Christians as "worrying." Meriam being charged with apostasy was one reason for this. Another was a government edict banning the construction of new church buildings. The government's contention was that many Christians had left and therefore fewer church buildings would be needed. The church leaders argument was that new buildings would be needed as Christians moved to newly developed areas. Further, the leaders claimed that church attendances were rising as more people whose registration was Christian had started attending services together with their families.

Underlying the issues is religious registration, since the state claims to be using a count of people registered as Christians to impose restrictions on the number of church buildings; the more relevant number of actual attendees is overlooked.

The Nile flows serenely through Sudan; justice and respect for diversity do not.

Sudan's President stated that the country would respond to South Sudan's cessation by becoming a more Islamic state. It remains to be seen what effects this has in the longer term for the Christian communities and society as a whole. Will the pluralism deficit get worse? The next stop on our regional tour is a country that claims to be an Islamic state. As we shall see, some of its citizens question whether it is truly so. It raises the question of what it means to be an Islamic country.

Chapter 12

Iran – an Islamic state?

Iran is a nation with a long and proud history and a rich culture. It is the nation with the earliest recorded use of the concept that we know as religious registration, as we saw in chapter 4. Today, the country still operates such a system.

Iran's population of more than 70 million is diverse. Religiously, an estimated 89% are Shi'ite Muslims, 9% are Sunni Muslims and 2% other faiths, including Baha'is, Christians, Jews, Mandeans and Zoroastrians. Sufi brotherhoods are popular, though there is no reliable demographic data. Ethnically, the Sunni are Arabs, Baluchs, Kurds and Turkmen. The Baluchs live mostly in the south-east near the border with Pakistan, with the Arabs mostly in the south-west close to Iraq, and the Kurds and Turkmen mostly in the north-west near the borders with Iraq and Turkey. The Shi'a are predominantly ethnically Persian, but also include Azeris, who constitute the second largest ethnic group in Iran, approximately 25% according to some estimates.

The Armenian and Assyrian (Chaldean) ethnic communities are recognised as Christians and preserve their own linguistic and cultural traditions. They have recognised churches conducting worship in their own languages, and can conduct marriages, i.e. they are millets.

Prior to mid-2011, a number of these Churches also conducted services in Farsi, often on Fridays, the main day of worship, as well as on Sundays. Since late 2011 the government has imposed severe restrictions, prohibiting Farsi language services and checking that those attending Armenian and Assyrian church services are ethnically Armenian or Assyrian. These checks are carried out on the basis of people's identity cards with the authorities recording attendees' names and identity card numbers which are then checked against the government's records.

In addition to the churches for the recognised indigenous Christian communities, there were also a number of (mostly Protestant) denominations that were originally established by and for the expatriate community. Over time these churches have become authentically Iranian, increasingly conducting some services in Farsi as well as English and other languages. From 2012 onwards these churches have come under increasing pressure and most ceased conducting public services during 2013 and 2014.

Prior to 2012 the application forms for identity cards and passports allowed the applicant to state their religion. Some converts entered 'Christian.' This received a mixed reception, with some reporting that their applications were accepted, processed and the documents issued as expected; others reporting that officials refused to accept their applications. Consequently, the authorities checking those attending church services could not simply look at the religious affiliation stated on citizens' identity cards; they needed to access government computer systems to check people's religious registration. A subtle point here is that an individual's self-identification of their religious affiliation on an identity card application does not change their religious registration as held by the government.

Iran has a unique governance structure based on the principle of Wilayat-al-Faqih, literally 'Guardianship of the Jurists.' Technically speaking, it is the only theocratic state on the planet. The head of state is The Supreme Ruler, currently Ali Khamenei. Very few people have the combination of in-depth Islamic legal expertise and acute political acumen to fulfil this post well. The President, currently Hassan Rouhani who was elected to this office in 2013, is the head of government. He nominates the cabinet, although the appointments must be approved by the Majlis, i.e. Parliament, which is an elected body. The Supreme Ruler holds far more power than the President. Several supervisory bodies hold these post holders and the Majlis to account, with the whole governance structure designed to protect and enshrine the Islamic revolution of 1979.

In the revolution of 1979, the Pahlavi dynasty, whose kings took the title of Shah, was overthrown. Ayatollah Khomeni returned from exile to become the head of state, and a new constitution and governance structure was inaugurated.

In 2009 a series of protests erupted when the results of a Presidential election were disputed. These became known as the Green Movement protests. During these protests many Iranians issued statements such as "this government is not truly Islamic," "this is the Shah with a different label" and "what we long for is a truly Islamic state, not the repressive one we have at present." In chapter 10 we remarked on Jeremy Bowen's observation that many revolutions ultimately end with something similar to that which the instigators set out to replace. Is Iran's 1979 revolution an example? As elsewhere, such comments raise the question of what it means to be Islamic or Muslim. We will address this question in the next chapter.

We can understand from where such a critique originates if we look at what Iran's constitution actually says about how the Islamic nature of the state is to be applied in practice to its citizens.

First, Article 12 states that there is to be respect for all schools of Islam. In practice, this is not what Sunnis and Sufis experience.

Second, Article 13 provides recognition of Christian, Jewish and Zoroastrian communities, "who, within the limits of the law, are free to perform their religious rites and ceremonies, and to act according to their own canon in matters of personal affairs and religious education." This provides the constitutional basis for the religious registration system. Schools for the Armenian community are permitted to include Christian religious education within the curriculum. However, such classes are frequently taught by teachers who are Muslims, a fact that is resented by many Armenian community and religious leaders.

Third, Article 14 obliges Muslims to treat non-Muslims "in conformity with ethical norms and the principles of Islamic justice and equity, and to respect their human rights." The Baha'i community in particular consistently complain that this provision is not upheld.

Fourth, Article 23 states, "The investigation of individuals' beliefs is forbidden, and no one may be molested or taken to task simply for holding a certain belief." This provision is violated in numerous cases in which Iranians have been arrested because of their Christian faith or activities.

Given the difference between the theory and the practice, it is no surprise that the Green Movement produced the critique mentioned above. Is Iran an Islamic state? It would appear that the answer varies according to who one asks, including amongst Iranians.

In January 2012 a major revision of the Penal Code completed its legislative passage and became law when signed by the President on 1st June 2013. Proposals presented to the Majlis in 2008 that explicitly criminalised apostasy were not included. We need to note that Article 220 provides explicitly that in the case of *hudud*, i.e. crimes, which are not explicitly covered by the Penal Code, judges are referred to Article 167 of the Constitution which provides that, if there is no codified law with respect to a particular issue, judges must deliver their judgments on the basis of authoritative Islamic sources, i.e. Shari'a and fatwa. Article 221 provides that, whenever it is necessary to refer to Article 167 in this way, judges must seek the advice of the office of The Supreme Leader, who may delegate that responsibility to others. This provision is designed to ensure some level of consistency in the application of Shari'a which is not formally encoded into legislation. In chapter 22 we will see an example of where the absence of such a provision causes serious concerns within society. The effect of these provisions is to formally establish the previous understanding, whereby the death penalty can be applied for apostasy through reference to Islamic sources.

It is rare for the formal charge of apostasy to be issued. Verbal threats of doing so, together with the closely associated threat of execution, is all too common. One example of this is described by Maryam Rostampour and Marziyeh Amirizadeh in their book *Captive in Iran*. They were detained for nine months during 2009 because of their faith and Christian activities. As with Meriam in Sudan, these two ladies were released following a world-wide public awareness campaign as well as discreet political pressure on the government.[17]

One example of where the actual charge of apostasy was issued concerns Pastor Yousef Nadarkhani of the

---

[17] Maryan Rostampour & Marziyeh Amirizadeh; *Captive in Iran*; (Tyndale, 2013) page 288, see also pages 255 and 273

Full Gospel Church of Iran. He was arrested on 12th October 2009 after complaining to the authorities that Christian children were forced to receive Islamic instruction in schools. This is a religious registration issue in itself – the parental norm of deciding on the religious education of their children being overridden. We have seen this before on our tour (the twins in Egypt) and will do so again in chapter 21.

In December 2010 the Revolutionary Tribunal of Gilan Province issued its official written verdict that they had found Yousef guilty of apostasy and so sentenced him to death. An appeal was submitted to the Supreme Court. On 22nd June 2011 Yousef's lawyers were informed verbally that the Supreme Court had rejected the appeal. However, in early July, and before the written verdict was issued, they were informed that the Supreme Court had returned the case to the Provincial Revolutionary Tribunal in order for the Tribunal to confirm whether Pastor Yousef had been a practising Muslim following attainment of the age of responsibility (i.e. 18) and before converting to Christianity. The Supreme Court also confirmed that Yousef would be acquitted should he recant his Christian faith. In Sudan, Meriam was given a specific timeframe of three days in which to recant; Yousef was given regular reminders that he had what the authorities regarded as a simple solution to his detention!

A series of hearings were held in Rasht from 25th to 28th September 2011. Pastor Yousef refused to recant. Although the court affirmed Yousef's claim not to have been a practising Muslim as an adult, the judge ruled that because he was of Muslim ancestry he remained guilty of apostasy as per the court's previous ruling. Note that in this case Yousef's beliefs and practices were not deemed to be relevant; it was his ancestry that decided the judge's verdict. The court never issued this verdict in writing. Yousef's lawyer was informed in October that the case was being referred to The Supreme Leader, and government officials announced that the Supreme Court would be willing to consider a further appeal if requested to do so.

On 4th July 2012 Yousef was verbally informed that he would face a fresh trial on new charges during September. No new charges were specified, and no indication was given that the previous conviction for apostasy would be overturned. A written summons was issued in late July, confirming the hearing as 8th September but not stating the purpose of the hearing. At the hearing, the apostasy charge was withdrawn.

However, Yousef was charged with evangelistic activities, convicted and sentenced to three years' imprisonment. He had already been detained for two years and 11 months and was immediately released on bail.

There was a further brief period of overt pressure from the authorities. In November 2012 two policemen visited the family home in Rasht with an arrest warrant for Yousef, citing charges of evangelistic activity. Yousef was outside Iran at the time, having recently spoken publicly at a meeting in the West. On 8th December he returned to Rasht. The director of Lakan prison, at which he had been detained, reportedly claimed that Yousef should have served some additional days before his release in September and summoned him to return to the prison to serve those additional days. This development was viewed by Yousef as an intimidatory tactic intended to force him to leave the country. In mid-December he was obliged to report to the prison each day. On 25th December he was detained. He was released on 7th January 2013, with orders to report back to the prison after 30 days in order to complete some paperwork. This duly happened. There have been no further official procedures against Pastor Yousef.

An earlier case involving an apostasy charge concerned lay church leader Hamid Pourmand. He was arrested on 9th September 2004 along with all 86 attendees at the Annual Meeting of the Assemblies of God Churches in Iran. 76 were released later the same day and nine pastors were released on the 12th leaving only Hamid detained. On 16th February 2005 he was formally convicted of deceiving the Iranian army about his conversion. The judge dismissed documents given him by Hamid showing that his superiors knew of his conversion before promoting him. He was sentenced to three years in prison plus dishonourable discharge from the army with immediate loss of all benefits. The next month he was formally charged with apostasy. A series of hearings followed during April. International attention to the case led first to these hearings being suspended and then moved from Tehran to Bandar-i Bushehr. The new judge was told to drop the charges, but refused and on 28th May he acquitted Hamid of the apostasy charge! Hamid was transferred back to Evin jail in Tehran. He was released in July 2006.

Of note here is that Hamid was treated differently from the other detainees because his religious registration was Muslim; all others were registered as

Christians. If Hamid's evidence is accepted then it would appear that the state (i.e. his employer) promoted him based on his competence whilst aware of and accepting his conversion. Only when his conversion came to prominence did a different branch of government exhibit a markedly different attitude towards his conversion and his employer apparently withdrew its support.

Since Hamid's case ended in 2006 and Yousef's in 2012, the pressures on Christians from Muslim backgrounds in Iran have risen. A number are detained, with several formally sentenced to jail terms of six years because of their Christian activities.

Some of the pressures and restrictions faced by Christians and by converts to Christianity have been outlined in this chapter. The same pressures, and at times worse, are faced by other religious minority groups, including Sunni and Sufi Muslim groups, and others such as Baha'is. Article 14 of the constitution might state that Muslims are to treat non-Muslims with due respect but this is not being upheld. We might ask how the authorities view the constitution's provisions for non-Muslims and how they determine who is Muslim or otherwise; do they apply citizens' religious registration or do they recognise people's religious beliefs and practices?

The first recorded use of what has come to be religious registration was in Iran. The original intent was to respect and honour all groups within society. Today, the system continues, but does not appear to respect, honour and affirm the contribution of all ethnic-religious groups within a harmonious whole. There is a distinct pluralism deficit.

We will pause our regional tour to look at these, and other, questions. Our context will be how religious registration underlies apostasy within criminal law. Our tour will then resume in Israel.

Chapter 13

Apostasy – leaving what?

We have described the cases of Meriam in Sudan and Yousef in Iran who were formally convicted of apostasy and sentenced to death.

Apostasy is defined as "leaving Islam." What an apostate becomes, Christian, Hindu, atheist, etc., is irrelevant. It raises the questions of who is a Muslim, how does one become a Muslim, and how does being a Muslim affect one's beliefs and behaviour?

Yousef argued that he was not an apostate because he had never held Islamic beliefs or participated in Muslim religious practices. This was confirmed by Iran's legal system, but treated as irrelevant. The state argued that he had been born to a father whom they regarded as a Muslim and so *de-facto* he was Muslim.

Likewise, Meriam never held Islamic beliefs or participated in Muslim worship. However, she was convicted on the basis that her father was registered as a Muslim, so therefore she was Muslim, even though the father abandoned the family when Meriam was six. Evidence from her childhood was either not available or disregarded.

For Yousef, the apostasy charge was simply dropped. For Meriam, her conviction was dismissed by an appeal court. Of note is that the court did so on procedural grounds. One wonders why the court did not order a retrial. In both cases, these decisions within the legal system followed a world-wide public awareness campaign.

What is the relevance of religious belief and practice in the legal processes applied in these cases? It matters for determining that Yousef and Meriam were not Muslims at the time of their trials; their self identification as Christians is accepted and their religious practices including regular church attendance were duly noted. Yousef, remember, is a pastor. However, belief and practice were irrelevant for determining whether they were Muslims at some point in the past. This is inconsistent.

Within religious registration systems, who is regarded as a Muslim is clear. Most are assigned that registration at birth. Most Middle Eastern countries allow those of other registrations to convert to Islam and have their registrations amended. The process is a legal one and usually comprises the making of a confession of faith before suitable witnesses. It is a single transaction process, i.e. what religious practice and refinement of beliefs follow is irrelevant. Once someone is a Muslim in this sense, then, in most countries, that is what they will remain; they cannot leave in the sense of changing their registration to another faith. (The exceptions that we have noted are Lebanon and Turkey – which allow anyone to switch their registration – and Egypt – which will allow people to reconvert to Christianity.)

In the case of Siham's husband, only the testimony of the witnesses mattered. It is clear that he never signed a 'conversion' certificate and it is also clear that there is no evidence that he ever practised as a Muslim. So, there is no evidence other than the word of the 'witnesses' that he made such a confession of faith.

In Egypt we noted that changes can occur due to administrative error. A long legal struggle ensued before those affected could have these errors quickly and efficiently corrected.

Meriam, Yousef and Hamid were subjected to a legal process within the criminal justice system which imposed the death penalty. Meriam and Yousef were pressed to recant their Christian faith. Views within Islam vary on the punishment for apostasy. Most sources do not apply the death penalty to women, only to men. Sudan takes the less common position and applies the death penalty to all. Most also say that one should be given three opportunities to recant – which is probably the basis on which Meriam was given three days to consider her situation. In Egypt, the typical view is that apostates should be given the rest of their lives to reconsider, and then let God deal with them, which is a justification for why apostasy is not criminalised in Egyptian law. In all these cases the element of individual choice of religion is present. We have seen cases in which some people's religious registration was changed as a consequence of a decision made by someone else. This includes Siham's children (chapter 1) and the twins in Egypt (chapter 2).

A further category of "conversion" is forced conversion. In July 2014 there were credible reports that the self-declared Islamic State was forcing some Christians to convert under the threat of death in parts of Iraq. Many chose to leave the area, becoming internally displaced persons (IDPs) elsewhere in Iraq. However, some elderly people were unable to travel. At least one such person was carried into a mosque, forced to say the Islamic creed and then informed that she was now part of the Muslim community. In this situation, there is no doubt that if she had refused to say the creed then there would have been serious consequences for her and the family members caring for her. It seems equally clear that her religious beliefs had not changed. A 'legal,' at least in some sense, process had taken place and been duly witnessed. Belief and practice is seemingly irrelevant. One unknown is whether her religious registration, as authenticated by the internationally acknowledged government of Iraq, has been changed. Will the government recognise the forced change or not?

In the history of religion in the Middle East, this is but the latest example of forced conversion. Islam is not the only religion some of whose adherents have perpetrated such acts. One wonders what such a conversion actually means? This is a question to which we will return shortly.

In passing we will ask who accepts that "The Islamic State" is actually Islamic. In the previous chapter on Iran we noted that some Iranians had questioned whether their country was truly Islamic. The Islamic State regards Iran as an apostate state, since Shi'a Muslims are not, in their eyes, Muslims at all. Likewise, the Islamic state is regarded by many

Muslims as not part of Islam. For example, in August 2014 the Grand Mufti of Saudi Arabia, the acknowledged leader of Islam in that country, stated that the Islamic State was public enemy number one.[18] In February 2015 King Abdullah of Jordan was quoted as saying that they should not be regarded as part of orthodox Islam and should not be referred to by their declared name. He used the term Daesh, which is a rough acronym and is seen as derogatory because it sounds like the Arabic word *daes* meaning to crush underfoot. King Abdullah refers to Daesh as *khawarij*, outlaws or renegades, and notes that they were looking for a legitimacy that they do not have inside orthodox Islam by being provocative towards the West.[19] Daesh have no doubt that they are Islamic, being explicit in citing early Islamic texts to justify all aspects of their actions. King Abdullah's view appears to be based on Daesh's rejection of all Islamic scholarship from the eighth century onwards. It raises

[18] E.g. Reuters; 19th August 2014; http://in.reuters.com/article/2014/08/19/iraq-security-saudi-mufti-idINKBN0GJ12420140819 (accessed 5th August 2015)
[19] Washington Post; 26th February 2015; http://www.washingtonpost.com/opinions/an-ideological-war-america-must-watch-not-fight/2015/02/26/6290938c-bdf8-11e4-bdfa-b8e8f594e6ee_story.html?hpid=z3 (accessed 27th February 2015)

the question of who is qualified to say what is Islamic and what is not.

It is pertinent to ask in what sense "The Islamic State" is a state? Clearly, it has control of some territory in which it provides a governance structure, public services and a justice system. There is no agreement as to what its borders are, and one cannot envisage it ever sending an ambassador to the UN or even neighbouring states. Daesh is a further example of names being problematic and revealing (see chapter 10).

In this context we should note that most Muslims find Daesh's behaviour repulsive. To most Muslims, "there should be no coercion in religion" (Shura 2:256). Many interpret this as meaning that there should be no coercion to become Muslim; it does not apply to those who are Muslims becoming adherents of another faith or none.

Apostasy raises the question of whether religious adherence is a personal choice or an aspect of a community's shared sense of identity. In other terms, what is the balance between individuals and communities in religious matters? We will return to these questions in chapter 27 when we look at international norms for religious freedom in the context of other types of rights including the freedom of conscience, expression and assembly.

Formally defined, religion is "a set of organised beliefs about the relationship between the natural and supernatural aspects of reality, and the role of human beings in this relationship." I like the colloquial version, "all that matters is not matter," a play on the two meanings of the word 'matter,' i.e. significance and physical material. In these definitions one significant element is the view that there is a supernatural dimension to reality that is accessible and relevant. Where is this aspect of religion in religious registration? We have noted at several points that belief and practice are irrelevant. A common element of Christianity and Islam is that human existence survives physical death where there is a separation in which some enter heaven and some do not. Many strands within Judaism have a similar concept, although we note that the Sadducees in New Testament times did not share this. Yet, the criteria for God's decision on entry to heaven and the extent to which adherents can be assured of what God will decide about them varies considerably, both across and also within each of these three monotheistic religions.

Nik Ripken in his book *The Insanity of God* gives an example where the assurance that some Christians have about the eternal destiny of their loved ones is clearly seen by Muslim friends present at the funeral of a 16 year old Christian child. The Muslim mourners are left asking why Christianity can have what is known as its "doctrine of assurance" when Islam offers no such assurance.[20]

The implications for Islam are profound. When someone becomes a Muslim, they hope that God regards their life as acceptable and trust for his mercy, although they have no assurance of being accepted by God. When extremists participate in the forced conversion of others they can claim to be enrolling people into the Muslim community but they cannot claim to be ensuring that the converted will enter heaven. It is presumed that they hope that God will look favourably on their own actions and count it to their credit. Their actions are primarily about their own eternal destiny.

[20] Nik Ripken; *The Insanity of God*; (B&H Publishing, 2013) pages 133-134

Within Christian communities, many use terms such as 'nominal' and 'believer' to differentiate between those whose loyalty to their religion consciously affects how they live. We might say that the term 'nominal' means those whose religious registration is Christian but who do not participate in regular worship even when they are able to do so. In contrast, the term 'believer' means those Christians who seek to demonstrate their loyalty to Jesus Christ by being regular in worship and living according to the teachings of their faith at all times and in all places. Their faith affects the whole of their character and actions.

There are similar differentiations and discussions within Judaism and Islam. Within Islam there is the "greater jihad" and the "lesser jihad." The greater jihad is the struggle to live appropriately. This is an inner struggle in which every Muslim is called to engage. The lesser jihad concerns the proclamation of the faith to non-Muslims. There is a wide range of views with one extreme being the use of violent means to forcibly convert others. This is the minority position, but typically attracts the most media attention.

We need to note one other form of apostasy seen within Islam, namely some Muslims regarding other Muslims as not true adherents. A typical example is Sunnis condemning Shi'a, of which Daesh is an extreme example. We should be aware that the same issue occurs within Christianity and in past centuries it has led to violent conflict. Today, it takes the form of lack of acceptance, recognition or trust. In Islam today there is a breadth of different practices with some embracing the diversity to the point of Sunni-Shi'a marriages and others regarding those with a different understanding of Islam as *infidels*, i.e. non-believers.

Returning to Christianity, we need to remind ourselves that there has been much discussion on what is appropriate in evangelism, i.e. in inviting non-Christians to become followers of Jesus Christ, with due adjustment to their religious beliefs and practices. Christianity is an evangelistic religion, as is Islam. In 2009 the Christian-Muslim Forum in the UK produced *Ethical Guidelines for Christian and Muslim Witness in Britain*. This emphasises that choice of religion is primarily a decision between the individual and God and that witness is by attitudes, actions and lifestyle as well as by words.[21]

Returning explicitly to apostasy and apostates, one caveat is worth noting. For those who become apostates by choosing to become Christians, we need to be aware that how they live is deeply significant. This is not easy, as illustrated by Brother Andrew and Al Janssen's book *Secret Believers*.[22] Acting in what is perceived by others as a deceitful manner usually results in a strong negative reaction. One illustration of this is the story of Baha in Egypt.

On 6th April 2005 Baha was arrested after speaking about his conversion to Christianity at a meeting in Alexandria. In July 2006 he was released but immediately re-arrested and moved to a different prison. He was released again on 28th April 2007. At one point during these two years he informed a judge that he regarded himself as a good Muslim now in contrast with having been a bad Muslim when he was a member of an extremist group, albeit one that

[21] Available on-line at http://www.christianmuslimforum.org/images/Ethical_Guidelines_for_Witnessv10.pdf (accessed December 2014)
[22] Published by Hodder & Stoughton in 2007

shunned violent methods. Baha was taking the word Muslim at its literal meaning of 'one who submits to God.' The judge reacted harshly, informing Baha not to be deceitful, using words to the effect of "it is fine to leave Islam, but don't pretend to be a Muslim when you have chosen to become an adherent of another faith."

Yousef and Meriam argued that they had never been Muslims. In chapter 1 we noted that Ramzi told a judge that he had been an agnostic before becoming a Christian and hence had never been a Muslim. The judge reacted harshly to what he saw as deceit. Underlying these reactions is the fact that religious registration is not about religious belief and practice. Meriam, Ramzi and Yousef were accurate in their view of never having been practicing Muslims. However, the religious registration systems applicable to each of them were very clear that before the law, the court and the judge they were registered as Muslims. Before such judges, self-identification of religious affiliation is recognised when it applies to having become a Christian but not when it applies to never having been Muslim in the sense of religious belief and practice.

Deceit usually results in a strong response when it is exposed. Those with religious registration of Muslim who become Christians need to be very careful in not being perceived to be acting deceitfully in the eyes of those in authority. David Garrison's book *A Wind in the House of Islam* documents the increasing numbers of such people in the twenty-first century.[23]

We conclude this chapter by noting that religious registration underlies apostasy being treated as a crime. The question of what makes one an adherent of a particular religion is debated within all faiths, as is the balance between personal and communal aspects of religious practice, affiliation and identity. Our tour moves to Israel, a country where the linkage of an ethnicity and a religion is rooted in history and has profound implications for many citizens, to the extent for some that it is not clear whether they are 'citizens' in its fullest sense.

[23] Published by Wigtake in 2014

Chapter 14

Israel – Jewish state or secular state?

In this chapter we look at Israel, whose religious registration system contains a number of distinct features. In the next leg of our regional tour we will look at the West Bank and Gaza Strip, where a significant adjustment was made to its religious registration system in February 2014.

Israel often describes itself as a Jewish state or as the state for the Jewish people. In chapter 10 we remarked that labels can be problematic and also revealing. What is meant by being a 'Jewish state?' Many of Israel's people are ethnically Jewish, 30% of whom were born abroad. Hebrew is widely spoken, as are Russian, Amharic (the language of the majority of Ethiopians), English and other languages, reflecting the countries of origin of many who have chosen to move to Israel and become Israeli citizens.

But Israel's population is not exclusively Jewish. Israeli Arabs comprise, according to Israel's Central Bureau of Statistics, 21% of the population. Religiously, these people are Muslim, Christian and Druze. They use Arabic as their mother tongue, with many also being fluent in Hebrew and English. Israeli Arabs complain of unfair treatment and being treated as *residents* rather than *citizens*. Some describe themselves as Palestinian, choosing to identify with those resident in the West Bank and Gaza Strip.

Four percent of the population are classified as 'other' within government statistics, i.e. they are not classified as Jew or Arab. This includes migrant workers (many of whom are Christian), asylum seekers and those whose status as Jewish is disputed. The state of Israel has been reasonably generous to asylum seekers, most of whom are African and enter by crossing the border from the Sinai Peninsula. Israel is currently constructing a fence along that border in order to restrict the entry of further migrants seeking asylum.

Israel's religious registration system is derived from the Ottoman era with adaptations during the British mandate era (i.e. 1918-1947) and more recent developments. A unique feature is that for a child born to parents with different registrations then the child's registration is that of the mother. Typically, this occurs within the Christian communities where the registration is specific to the church denomination.

There are 14 recognised ethnic-religious groups, each of which operates a system of religiously based courts that have exclusive control over marriage and divorce. Marriage is exclusively within religious legal systems – a situation that informs one of the many political debates within Israeli society as some call for the addition of civil marriage whilst others strive to maintain the status quo. This debate has led to one adjustment which we will discuss later.

Matters such as custody and inheritance are handled in religious and civil courts, with most citizens having a choice as to which system will be applied in their situation. This is different from other Middle Eastern countries where there are fewer, if any, civil options.

One difference from the Ottoman era is that the Druze have a millet. Another is that all 14 religious groups have the same standing before the government. In contrast, under the Ottomans the Muslim millet had precedence with the word of a Muslim carrying twice the weight as the word of a member of another millet.

Jewish, Druze and Christian families may ask for some personal status cases, including alimony and child custody, to be adjudicated in civil courts. In cases of divorce, Jewish women are subject to the exclusive jurisdiction of the rabbinical courts if their spouses file the case there first. Since 2001 Muslim women may file cases related to custody, alimony, or property division associated with divorce in civil courts. In practice, however, societal pressures frequently prevent Muslim women from using this option. Some couples who marry in the country, including Catholics, cannot get a divorce unless they change their religious registration to a religious authority that authorises divorce.

Within the religious registration system, it is presumed that those who are ethnically Jewish are followers of Judaism. This is a subtle and deliberate linking of the ethnicity with the religion, based on the history of the Jewish people. Consequently, Jewish citizens' personal status matters are handled within a court system based on Judaism, irrespective of the actual beliefs and religious practices of the individual(s) concerned.

Some conversions receive a degree of official recognition. This was illustrated on 17th August 2014 when a Jewish woman married an Israeli Arab man. The lady changed her religious registration to Muslim prior to the wedding. Their wedding was marked by two sets of demonstrators, one opposed to the marriage and the other supportive. Of note is that the couple could not do the opposite, i.e. the man would not have been able to change his registration to match that of his bride.

Changing their religious registration is possible for many of the non-Jewish citizens. For Christians wishing to become Muslims the change is relatively straightforward. For Muslims wanting to become Christians the change is not impossible, although it is complex and far from common. Most people who convert simply leave their registration unchanged.

The Ministry of Religious Affairs has jurisdiction over the country's 133 Jewish religious councils which oversee the provision of religious services for Jewish communities. Legislation establishing religious councils includes the Druze but excludes other non-Jewish communities. The Ministry of the Interior has jurisdiction over religious matters concerning non-Jewish groups, while the Ministry of Tourism is responsible for the protection and upkeep of non-Jewish holy sites.

How do we interpret the titles of these three government ministries? Religious Affairs is restricted to Judaism, with other religions diverted elsewhere. Are they not religions? Does being overseen by the Interior Ministry imply that they are being treated as potential enemies within the state, requiring close scrutiny by the security services? Do non-Jewish holy sites being overseen by the Ministry of Tourism imply that these sites are for visitors rather than citizens? Are these contributory factors to Israeli Arabs' view that they are treated as *residents* rather than true *citizens*?

A subtle aspect of this arrangement is the treatment of the Druze community, whose affairs are handled in a similar manner to the Jewish communities, and distinctly different from other non-Jewish ethnic-religious communities. This dates back to the 1950s when Druze community leaders encouraged their young people to enlist for national service. They have participated in all military duties, and some suggest that the casualties suffered are proportionately higher than for Jewish people. Druze communities have derived some benefits, notably job opportunities, from such overt loyalty to the state. Their sense of identity remains firmly Druze, even if they have reduced their sense of Arab identity and increased their sense of being Israeli citizens.

In September 2014 the Minister of the Interior formally authorised the use of the term "Aramean" as a distinct ethnic identity that could now be used on official documents. The decision allowed 200 Israeli Arab families to use this designation for themselves. Critics argued that the measure was part of a campaign by the authorities to split the Israeli Arab community on religious lines, i.e. Christians and

Muslims, Arameans being part of Israel's Christian communities. Part of this campaign is to encourage Israeli Arab Christians to serve in the military, a programme that has proven to be controversial within the Christian community. It is seen by some as asking people to choose between their Israeli citizenship and Arab ethnicity, two aspects of their sense of identity. The government rewards those who undertake national service with a number of benefits, including financial support for higher education.

In 2000 the government enacted a law that ordered businesses not to discriminate on the basis of gender, religion, colour, ethnicity or sexual orientation in any aspect of their activities, such as employment practices, customer services and supplier contracts. This measure endeavoured to improve social cohesion across the diversity of society. It can be viewed as supporting a pluralist approach to governance. However, the measure is specific to businesses; government services continue to vary across ethnic communities.

Israel operates the "Law of Return", which grants the right of those regarded as Jewish to immigrate to Israel and receive citizenship. Those who exercise this right are said to be "making aliya." The original (1950)

Law of Return did not define who was considered a Jew. An amendment in 1970 enacted two changes to the law seeking to clarify this aspect of the law. Section 4A(a) extends the right of return to:

> "a child and a grandchild of a Jew, the spouse of a Jew, the spouse of a child of a Jew and the spouse of a grandchild of a Jew, except for a person who has been a Jew and has voluntarily changed his religion."

Section 4B seeks to clarify the definition of who is a Jew. It states that:

> "For the purpose of this Law, 'Jew' means a person who was born of a Jewish mother or has become converted to Judaism and who is not a member of another religion."

The reference to those who have chosen to follow another religion can be significant, as we will see later in this chapter.

In practice, there are problems caused by inconsistencies between the religious establishment and government ministries in the definition of who qualifies as *Jewish* and who does not. This causes serious problems for some due to the religious establishment's exclusive control over marriages, conversions and in some cases burial rights. It should be noted that many Jewish citizens object to the exclusive control of marriage by the religious authorities. Such people seek a civil option as a complement to the religious system.

One motivation is to address the anomaly that leaves an estimated 300,000 Israeli citizens unable to marry in Israel. These people are Israeli citizens whose claims to being Jewish are rejected by the religious authorities controlling Judaism. One option available to these citizens is to marry abroad because the state authorities will recognise such a marriage. This means that they are not coerced into adopting another religion in order to find a court system willing and able to conduct a marriage ceremony. In 2012 the government sought to address this situation by enacting a law to cover marriage for "those with no religion." This allows Israeli citizens unable to marry within a religious system to apply to the Ministry of the Interior in order to register a marriage.

It would be more accurate to term this as covering those with "no religion that is *recognised by the state.*" This distinction is significant to some Christians, notably Evangelical Protestants. These churches are not recognised as a denomination, and so cannot operate a religious court system and hence cannot, strictly speaking, conduct marriages. There is a long-standing ad-hoc arrangement to cover this which uses special forms issued by the Ministry of the Interior. The Ministry proposed withdrawing this system because those affected could use the new law. However, those Christians affected objected to this on the grounds that they clearly do have a religion, making it insensitive to force them to use an arrangement designated for those "having no religion." The Ministry listened to their concerns, and the previous arrangement continues to operate. The desire of the affected Christian communities is to be granted recognition as a denomination. The affected churches have formed a collective body and applied for such recognition. To date their request has not been granted.

One group pushing for civil marriage is the gay community. They are seeking same-sex marriage, as has been legalised in a number of Western countries. However, any such arrangement would have to be within a civil system since none of the religious communities would consider authenticating such marriages. Israel, as a secular state, grants significant recognition to couples cohabiting without being married. This includes being treated as if they were married within the tax system, and recognition of joint and combined assets. The state recognises the use of such provisions whenever they have been claimed by cohabiting homosexual couples.

The Jewish people trace their history to their patriarchs - Abraham, Isaac and Jacob. Membership of the community was largely based on direct descent from the twelve tribes named after the twelve sons of Jacob. This was adjusted when land was allocated, with the Levities being dispersed amongst the other tribes to serve as priests and the two sons of Joseph, Ephraim and Manasseh, allocated distinct territory.[24] The Hebrew Scriptures record the presence of non-Jews within the community at the crucial moment in the history of the Israelites, namely the Exodus from Egypt. Inclusion in the community was rooted primarily in allegiance to Yahweh, the God of the Israelites.[25] We noted earlier that religious registration in Israel follows the female line for all ethnic-religious groups. At what point in their history

[24] Genesis 48:5
[25] See Exodus 12:38a ("Many other people went up with them")

does being an Israelite switch from being based on the paternal to the maternal line? The answer appears to lie in Jewish history, notably of forced displacement followed by exploitation and marginalisation in many of the locations to which they were dispersed. It was always clear who a baby's mother was but not always clear who the father was, notably in situations where women had been sexually abused by conquerors.

Judaism in Israel is diverse. On 14th August 2013 Yitzhak Yosef and David Lau were sworn in as Chief Rabbis by the then President Peres. The country has two Chief Rabbis; one serving Ashkenazi Judaism and the other Sephardi Judaism. (See appendix 1 for the origins of this diversity.) The President urged the new Chief Rabbis to use their positions to help heal the rifts in Israeli society, especially between those who are religiously observant and those less so.

The two Chief Rabbis form the Chief Rabbinate of Israel and alternate as president of the Chief Rabbinate Council. These bodies have responsibility for overseeing the millet for Jewish citizens. Having two Chief Rabbis raises the question of authority within Judaism. There is nobody entitled to speak on behalf of all adherents of Judaism whose authority is accepted by all communities. The same is true for Christianity and Islam.

Another group within Judaism that is attracting attention and some degree of political controversy is the Haredi community. This community has been referred to as the ultra-Orthodox. However, this term is falling into disuse because it is perceived to be derogatory and to imply extremism by some – another example of names being problematic. The literal meaning of Haredi is 'those who tremble before the word of God.' Typically, male members of this community spend their time exclusively on religious matters, living on state benefits in order to study Torah and Rabbinic writings. They insist on segregation from the rest of society, including having separate schools to prevent intermingling of their children with the rest of the population. They often have large families. A study by demographers at Haifa University published in November 2010 estimated that 30% of Jewish babies were born to Haredi families. Government statistics from a similar period state that 9% of the population were Haredim and this was predicted to rise to 15% by 2025. Haredim are seen by many of their fellow Israelis as a burden, or as a state-within-a-state, due to their living on benefits. The effect of this community on the government's welfare budget is an increasingly significant issue.

In 2013, Prime Minister Benjamin Netanyahu called an early general election. One reason was the difficulty in passing the government's national budget. Consequently, the financial costs of the Haredim became an election issue. Following the election and the formation of a new government a budget was passed which included significant changes in the handling of the Haredi community. They could retain their own schools, but state funding for them would be adjusted to reflect the extent to which they included the whole national curriculum. Many Israelis find that those raised in Haredi communities are unemployable because the entire curriculum has been focussed on religious studies. This is another way in which the Haredim are perceived to be a burden on the rest of Israeli society. The Haredi leaders respond that the state will benefit from the continuous study of Torah because this pleases God who will respond by blessing the nation. A secular state finds such an argument impossible to quantify.

The Haredi community is itself diverse. Some embraced the changed government funding of schooling and included a broader curriculum; others resisted and sought ways to maintain their previous practice. Another factor is the community's reluctance to serve in the military. On 21st February 2012 the Supreme Court ruled that the Tal Law, which gave Haredim an exemption from compulsory military service, was unconstitutional. No equivalent legislation was enacted, making members of the Haredi community liable for compulsory national service. Some Haredi groups allow their youth to respond to call-up papers, complying, even if reluctantly, whilst others encourage doing voluntary service, which is a recognised alternative. In contrast, some refuse to comply, ignoring call-up papers, effectively challenging the state to arrest and imprison people for following their religiously-based convictions. Is Israel a secular or a religious state?

In chapter 3 we noted that national law and religious law can come into conflict. Reaction to the removal of the Tal Law is one example of this. Another example began in 2006 when a bakery in Ashdod had its "kosher" certificate withdrawn purely because the Jewish owner had chosen to accept Jesus as the Messiah, i.e. had converted to Christianity. Such people commonly describe themselves within

Christian circles as "Messianic believers." The baker initiated court proceedings to challenge the religious discrimination. This process proved somewhat lengthy, as we saw earlier with legal cases in Jordan and Egypt.

On 29th June 2009 the High Court of Justice issued a 12-page ruling instructing the Chief Rabbinate of Israel (see Glossary) to grant the bakery a kosher certificate. The judges emphatically rejected the claims of the Chief Rabbinate's counsel that it is impossible to trust Messianic Jews to uphold their commitments before the Rabbinate since they are "apostate Jews." The judges described the Rabbinate's decision as "unreasonable, disproportionate" and "impossible to support." The use of the word 'apostate' in this context is interesting; an Islamic term has been adopted by Judaism to refer to someone leaving a community into which they were born. Also significant is the use of the term 'Jew.' The baker's ethnicity has not changed; what has changed is that he is clearly not an adherent of Judaism.

Alas, the Rabbinate did not issue the certificate. The baker started a second court case on the grounds that the Rabbinate was in contempt of court for refusing to act as instructed. During the ensuing legal battle it emerged that additional requirements had been introduced in order to qualify for a kosher certificate. The High Court demanded to see evidence that all bakeries in Ashdod were being treated equally.

The relevance to our topic is the use of religious law to override national and state law. Where religiously based legal codes are operative, problems will inevitably arise unless there are very clear boundaries to their jurisdiction and civil-based alternatives are available to those unwilling to accept the authority of religiously based systems.

This case has introduced the issues faced by Messianic believers. Legal process discrimination occurs for those whose allegiance to Yeshua is known. Yeshua is the Hebrew form of Jesus, although it would be more accurate historically to say that Jesus is the English form of Yeshua. They also experience many of the same issues with their family as do Yeshua's followers from Muslim backgrounds, i.e. ostracism, disinheritance and perceived disloyalty. The term 'apostate' appeared above. It is all too apt, at least socially and culturally. At least in Israel apostasy is not a crime.

Some Messianic believers encounter difficulties when they seek to marry. If their acceptance of Yeshua as Messiah is known to the Rabbinic authorities then some Rabbis refuse to conduct a wedding. Such Rabbis are treating the couple as apostates who are no longer Jewish and hence not within their jurisdiction. However, the couple do not come under any other religiously based court system, with the implication that they cannot marry in their own country.

A similar issue also affects members of branches of Judaism that are not recognised or accepted within the mainstream traditions. This is true for followers of Karaiti Judaism and for some Reform Jews (see Glossary). At the time of writing, some such groups were establishing, in some sense, their own court systems outside of the officially recognised structures overseen by the Chief Rabbinate of Israel. What authority the new bodies have outside of their own communities is debateable.

In recent years there have been several cases in which a Messianic believer attempting aliya under the Law of Return has been denied citizenship. Some of those so denied have sought legal redress, arguing that they remain Jewish in all ethnic, cultural and social senses whilst accepting Yeshua as their Messiah. This is one reason why many Messianic believers do not like being labelled with the term "Christian." They have no sense of crisis about their identity. However, others in Israel certainly do have a sense of conflict or crisis over such people's identity.

The Israeli Supreme Court is clear on this issue. The Law of Return excludes Jewish people who have chosen to become adherents of another faith. Of the various bodies that handle aliya, some do question applicants on their religious beliefs and practices, others do not. In general, the authorities in Israel itself rarely ask about such matters.

We end this chapter with a brief reflection on the city of Jerusalem, which holds significance for adherents of Judaism, Christianity and Islam. It is the location of the Western Wall, regarded as the holiest site in Judaism, and of the Dome of the Rock and al-Aqsa mosques, two revered sites within many Islamic traditions. Within Christianity, Jerusalem hosts a rich diversity of church groups. There are three Patriarchs, four Archbishops and five Bishops, plus numerous clergy and other church employees. In his book *Whose Holy City*, Colin Chapman points out that the history of Jerusalem includes 20 sieges, two ruinations, 18 reconstructions and at least 11 transitions of major religion.[26] Is any other city as religiously diverse?

Control of property and land within Jerusalem remains a constant source of friction, political manoeuvring and, occasionally, bitter legal disputes. Several long-standing churches have considerable property holdings in Jerusalem. The land on which the Knesset (the Israeli parliament) stands is owned by the Greek Orthodox Church. There have been occasions when the Israeli authorities delay the issuing of official recognition of senior clergy in order to put pressure on a particular denomination to agree to some property transactions.

The Greek Orthodox Church has at times been guilty of denigrating fellow Christians, asserting that the Greek tradition was superior because much of the New Testament was written in Greek. Consequently, some Israeli Arab Christians were being told that they were second class ethnically (because they were Arab) and second class religiously (because they were not of the Greek Orthodox tradition). Their sense of identity had multiple challenges.

---

[26] Colin Chapman; *Whose Holy City*; (Lion, 2004) page 8, citing Amos Elon, *Jerusalem: Battleground of Memory* (Kodansha America, 1995)

So is Israel a Jewish state or a secular state? Both, in some respects. The struggles over identity seem likely to continue, as will the struggles over the clear rule of law applied equally to all.

One area of conflict is the exclusive control of marriage by religious bodies, a battle that has left some Israeli citizens unable to marry in their own country. We will pause our tour of the region to reflect on the issue of marriage, one of the flash points in religious registration matters.

Chapter 15

Please Will You Marry Me?

We have already referred to this subject at several points. In the previous chapter we noted that a number of citizens cannot get married in their own country; their only option is to marry abroad. This situation occurs in several Middle Eastern countries.

What is all too common is the restriction that women who are registered as Muslim can only marry men with the same registration. A man, however, whose religious registration is Muslim is allowed to marry a woman whose religious registration is Christian or Jewish. The marriage automatically changes the woman's registration to Muslim. In some places and by some Muslims, men are encouraged to marry non-Muslims as a means of enlarging the Muslim community and reducing the number of babies born into non-Muslim communities. Jordan is an example of this, as we noted in chapter 8.

In our second visit to Egypt – chapter 9 – we looked at Martha's situation. She had converted to Christianity but was unable to change her registration. She was unable to legally marry the man she loved because his registration was Christian. This prompted her to illegally acquire identity documents stating that she was Christian. When this was discovered by the authorities it initiated a series of challenges that continue to this day with profound consequences for her and her family.

In Sudan – chapter 11 – we remarked on the situation of Meriam together with her husband Daniel and their family. Meriam was being regarded as having a religious registration of Muslim which meant that her marriage to Daniel was null and void before the state – although it remained valid in the eyes of the church.

We should keep in mind that marriage is both a relationship and a legal contract. For Martha and Meriam it is the legal contract aspect that their governments are treating as invalid.

In the previous chapter we noted that those Israelis unable to marry in their own country can get married abroad with their government recognising the marriage. Earlier in our tour we noted that the Lebanese government also fully respects marriages conducted abroad. So this option is available for some converts to Christianity who retain non-Christian religious registrations. However, it does not work for all.

The question of 'who can marry whom' can become very complex if the man and woman are of different nationalities as well as different religious registrations. It is of greater significance than when husband and wife have the same nationality since it affects residency rights, the nationality of any children and, in some countries, access to state benefits.

The international norm is that when people marry abroad their country's embassy or other official representation is informed of the marriage. This is due legitimate procedure. However, some Middle Eastern governments take note of the religious registration of those involved in such marriages and then apply their national legal criteria. One example is Egypt. They would regard the 'marriage' of a female Egyptian with a religious registration of Muslim as null and void if the man, of any nationality, had what they regarded as a registration other than Muslim. If the couple were subsequently to visit Egypt then they would be regarded as unmarried, since the legal contract aspect of their marriage is not recognised.

So in the case of Martha and her husband, if they had married abroad using her original identity documents they would, most likely, have faced serious problems when they returned to Egypt. They had no viable, legal option that their government would respect.

Marriage leads to the related issue of the raising of children. One aspect directly affected is their religious education. Normal practice in the Middle East is to provide both Islamic and Christian religious education classes, with pupils allocated according to their religious registration.

During our regional tour we have noted two instances where religious education in state schools caused problems. This is another flash point of religious registration. In our first visit to Egypt – chapter 2 – we noted the case of the twin boys whose forced change of religion came to public attention when they were moved from the Christian to the Islamic religious education class. In Sudan – chapter 11 – we noted that Meriam's school records were sought by her lawyer as a means of demonstrating that she was regarded by the state as a Christian during her childhood.

There is a generic problem here for couples both of whose registration is different from that of their actual beliefs. Two Christians from Muslim backgrounds can marry, often quite easily, although they must do so with an Islamic ceremony. Some are content to quietly accept this; others resent it intensely but have no alternative. Some are able to have a discreet Christian ceremony to complement the official legal process. However, circumstances do not always allow this. In the previous chapter we noted that Messianic believers encounter similar challenges with marriage if their conversion is known to religious officials.

When such couples have children they and their children are placed in the situation of regarding themselves as Christians at home but being treated as Muslims at school. Some handle this well, for others it has been known to cause major problems. A typical example is as follows. A child tells a classmate that his family are Christians. This is then reported to the classmate's parents who were unaware of the family being Christians. This leads to societal pressure and discrimination on the family as their religious allegiance becomes known having previously been maintained discreetly.

As we noted when discussing apostasy – chapter 13 – it is not always easy to live appropriately as a Christian whose religious registration is Muslim. It can be difficult to avoid being perceived as deceitful when the religious registration system and the associated societal norms do not allow overt recognition and acceptance of a changed religious belief.

We also need to touch on the ending of marriage in divorce. Some religious traditions permit divorce whilst others do not. Within Christianity, this varies from one denomination to another. Those who are members of a church that does not allow divorce sometimes choose to change their registration either to Islam or to another denomination that permits divorce. The case of the twins in Egypt is an example of the latter – their father left their mother and changed his registration to Muslim in order to marry a woman whose registration was Muslim.

Incidentally, note that we speak of people changing their registration, rather than 'converting.' The word convert implies a change of belief and practice. That is not necessarily the case here; he changed his registration in order to marry. We do not know whether he changed his beliefs and practices. We need to keep in mind that religious registration is not necessarily about belief and practice.

So marriage is a flash point of religious registration, especially for converts and for those wishing to marry someone with a different registration. In such cases, religious registration operates to the disadvantage of Christian, and other distinct non-Muslim, communities.

Chapter 16

Palestine – who governs what, where?

We continue our tour of the region with a look at the West Bank and Gaza Strip. It's worth our while to give a short description of the governance structures applicable in these areas to establish who has control of matters relevant to our primary focus on religious registration.

The Palestinian Authority was established by the Oslo Accords of 1993 as the governing body of those parts of the West Bank and Gaza Strip that would be transferred to Palestinian control. These Accords defined three types of control to be known as Area A, Area B and Area C. Area A would be under the full control of the Palestinian Authority; Area B would be under Palestinian administrative control but Israeli security control, meaning that Palestinian police forces need permission from the Israeli authorities to enter these areas; Area C would be under full Israeli control.

From 1993 onwards parts of the West Bank and Gaza Strip were duly transferred, beginning with the major population centres. In 2005 Israel completed the transfer of the Gaza Strip when it withdrew from its settlements and associated military bases. The whole of the Gaza Strip became Area A.

For the West Bank, 17% of the territory is Area A and just over half of the West Bank's Palestinian population live in such areas. 24% is Area B in which 41% of the Palestinians in the West Bank live. Area C includes the Israeli settlements and most of the Jordan valley. 59% of the West Bank is Area C, with 4% of the Palestinian West Bank population living there. Israel retains control of the airspace, most of the borders and the coastal waters of the Gaza Strip.

In practice, Israel maintains a strong interest even in Area A, with full control over imports, exports, the movement of people and telephony services. Its security services enter to conduct searches and arrests whenever the Israeli authorities deem it necessary.

So what role does the Palestinian Authority have? As one Palestinian leader explained to me, in effect, it is the dispenser of municipal services for the major Palestinian population centres. It has both legislative and administrative control over such matters.

In recent years there have been strong moves towards seeking official recognition of statehood. Former

Prime Minister Salim Fayyad took the view "if we want a state, we must build one." He actively sought to develop the Palestinian Authority's institutions to the point that they would be fit for purpose in a sovereign state.[27]

The Palestinian Authority operates a religious registration system within the West Bank and Gaza Strip. There are some links to the political system. Six of the 132 seats in the legislative assembly are reserved for Christians and the mayors of the towns of Beit Jala, Bethlehem and Ramallah are required to be Christian. There are no such provisions for any other faith.

Most demographic sources state that up to 2% of the Palestinian population are Christian. One credible source gives a figure of 1.1%. In 1967 the figure was 12%. Emigration of Christians is an issue throughout the Middle East. Nowhere is the demographic change so marked as it is here.

The religious registration system has changed little since the Ottoman era. There is one millet and

[27] Prime Minister Fayyad stated this on numerous occasions including a talk given in Bethlehem in March 2012 attended by the author.

religious court system for Muslims. Ten Christian denominations have full legal recognition and are regarded as competent to operate religious courts. Such denominations are the same as those recognised by the Ottoman Empire in the late nineteenth century. There are churches belonging to the Catholic, Eastern Orthodox, Oriental Orthodox and Protestant traditions.

A number of other denominations established prior to 1967 have unwritten status and are able to operate freely in terms of worship services. They are able to perform some personal status matters, notably being able to conduct officially recognised marriages. In addition, there are a number of newer denominations that can operate as churches but are not able to officially conduct personal status matters.

On 2nd February 2014 the Ministry of the Interior announced that religious registration would be removed from identity cards. This was duly implemented. Newly issued cards do not include the holder's religion. The system itself continues unchanged, with people's religious registration held on the authority's computer systems. Why was this change made?

The Palestine Basic Law, which functions like a constitution, was passed by the Palestinian Legislative Council (the parliament of the Palestinian Authority) and signed into law by the then President Yasser Arafat in 2002. It states that Islam is the official religion and Shari'a the main source of legislation. It includes numerous provisions on the rights of citizens, including that there should be no discrimination on the grounds of gender, ethnicity, political views or religion. The February 2014 announcement cited this "constitution-like" requirement as the reason for removing religious registration from identity cards.

The change can rightly be regarded as remarkable. It is the first authority to take this step (excluding Lebanon whose context is different from the rest of the region). We can note the contrast with Turkey (chapter 5) whose government stated they would do this but did not. Here, the authorities promptly implemented their stated intention. It has been warmly welcomed by those Muslims who have chosen to become Christians; many have applied for and received new identity cards.

During 2014 one Palestinian church leader remarked that "the authorities are treating Christians very well in general." He noted the authorities were acting to reduce the pressure exerted by extremists on Christians, citing the commitment to remove religious registration from identity cards as one example of this.

However, others noted that, in general, the rule of law is quite weak and there is some corruption within the justice system. Therefore, whether an individual has their rights upheld may depend more on who they know, or can bribe, as much as on the rights and wrongs of their case. In such circumstances it is usually the case that members of minority communities receive worse treatment than others.

Some suspect that there are elements of positive discrimination for Christians, notably in any matter that requires the approval of the Israeli authorities, such as travel permits between the Gaza Strip and the West Bank. Consequently, some wonder if the change in the identity cards was intended to make it more difficult for the Israeli authorities to discriminate on religious grounds in matters concerning Palestinians.

It is interesting to note that during 2011 there were a number of peaceful protests in the West Bank calling for an end to corruption. One reason for Hamas' electoral successes in 2006 and earlier was that they were regarded as trustworthy with resources.[28] This illustrates the awareness and disgust at corruption amongst the population, an awareness that is symptomatic across much of the Middle East. Hezbollah's popularity in Lebanon was likewise enhanced by its reputation for trustworthiness with resources. Tackling corruption was one aspect of former Prime Minister Fayyad's efforts to build credible institutions and his achievements in this area were recognised by the International Monetary Fund. The Arab Awakening touched the West Bank, although here there was no need for protestors to call for "democracy" since an electoral system is well established. One difficulty here is that the outcome of the Parliamentary election in 2006 was not respected by the Israeli government nor the governments of numerous other countries.

Religious conversion remains controversial within society. This was well illustrated by an incident in the Gaza Strip in July 2012. In two separate incidents a

[28] See for example Marwan Muasher; *The Second Arab Awakening and the Battle for Pluralism*; (Yale University Press, 2014) page 73 where he notes that support for Hamas was based on a desire a for good governance and tackling corruption.

man and a woman with her three children converted from Christianity to Islam and had their religious registration changed. Both left their homes and stayed with Muslim religious officials. Members of the Christian community claimed that these were forced conversions and that the man and woman were being held against their will. However, they both made public statements that they had acted voluntarily. On 19th July the man returned to his family after family members undertook to respect his choice. These incidents led to great stress in the Christian community in Gaza, who saw these conversions (and other alleged conversions) as the result of increasing social and economic pressure on members of their small community to convert to Islam. Some Christians are enticed into changing their religious registration to Muslim with the offers of jobs, houses, wives and diplomas. Such approaches are especially prevalent during Ramadan. Occasionally the approach is more violent.

There are three recognised church buildings in the Gaza Strip, namely, the Church of Saint Porphyrius (Eastern Orthodox), The Holy Family Catholic Church and the Gaza Baptist Church in an area that is home to more than 1,800,000 people.

Let us pause our regional tour to ask who is allowed – legally and culturally – to worship where. Following which, the next stop on our regional tour will be Iraq, a land in which forced conversion was practised in some parts during 2014, as we noted when we examined apostasy.

Chapter 17

May I worship with you?

As we have noted, in many Middle Eastern countries those with religious registration of Muslim who choose to become Christians cannot have their religious registration changed to match their choice of faith. How does this affect their ability to worship with others?

Church buildings are for Christians, mosques are for Muslims and synagogues are for followers of Judaism. Are places of worship available for everyone or only for those whose religious registration matches that of the place of worship? Also of relevance is when are such places open: just for previously announced services or at other times as places of prayer or pilgrimage?

One large church in a major city in the Middle East acknowledges that Muslims in the religious registration sense are welcome to attend. Size and scale assist them in this. Also significant is that major cities are frequently more cosmopolitan and pluralistic than towns and villages.

In contrast, in villages where typically most people know everyone else, someone attending a place of worship of a different faith from that of their registration will be observed, remarked about and in all likelihood acted upon. The individual will be quizzed about their action; the leader of the place of worship will be asked what that person was doing and why they were permitted to enter. In extreme cases, mob violence occurs, especially if a senior community figure publicly denounces such attendances. What has happened on occasions, notably in Egypt, is that a leader of a mosque informs his congregation that a local Muslim has been seen attending a church which acts as an incitement to some in the congregation to form a mob and attack the church or its priest. This is the third time that we have encountered the threat or use of mob violence in religious registration related matters – the first was in Egypt against individuals, communities (chapter 9) and church property (chapter 10) and then against Meriam in Sudan (chapter 11). Religious registration is being used to identify targets for the inappropriate expression of anger and underpins a sense of impunity for the perpetrators.

In these areas, societal expectations restrict people to worship based on their registration. Those that wish to change are obliged to move and live elsewhere. In extreme cases, they are obliged to move to another country. May I worship with you? In many locations, only if your registration matches the sign on the building.

Being able to attend worship services is important. Being fully accepted as a member of a specific religious congregation involves deeper issues. One pastor explained that those from Muslim backgrounds were welcome to attend his church and some came to be accepted as regular attendees and then participants. For some individuals, serious challenges emerge. One common area is whether such people can hold leadership positions? Frequently, this is denied, mainly due to concerns about how the authorities would respond.

Another area which often causes tension is marriage. Many Christian men are reluctant to allow their daughters to marry a man from a Muslim background, irrespective of how sincere they are in their commitment to Christ. The children of such a marriage will be regarded as Muslims. The case of Ramzi and Muna (chapter 1) illustrates the fear that the man's relatives could use this to seek custody of the children; if custody were lost then this would most likely deny the grandparents all access to their grandchildren. We noted in chapter 14 on marriage that the reverse is not possible, i.e. a woman registered as a Muslim cannot marry a Christian man.

A further area that can cause difficulties is the cultural differences between Christian and Muslim communities that are noticeable in many Middle Eastern countries. This can lead to misunderstanding and culture shock when those from one background join with those from a different background for worship.

This topic of who can worship with whom remains a crucial issue for many Christians in the Middle East. Some fear that it is pushing those from Muslim backgrounds to form new fellowships and churches which are exclusively for such people. Whilst the reasons for this are well understood, and agonised over, some desire a greater sense of inclusion within the long established Christian communities across the Middle East.

In Iran (chapter 12) we noted that the authorities overtly monitor church buildings to ensure that only those whose religious registration is Christian attend services. This level of scrutiny has forced all Christians to evaluate whether they are willing to be known as regular attendees at church services. May I worship with you? Only if you are willing to be publicly identified as a church attendee in the eyes of the state.

One effect in Iran has been to force those from Muslim backgrounds to meet in house fellowships. The Iranian government, like many others in the region, is suspicious of any activity in society that it cannot monitor and, if necessary, control. Therefore, any unofficial and independent movement can be regarded as a potential threat to the government's authority, with consequent attention by the security services.

Another area in which some governments impose undue restrictions concerns recognition of the diversity of expression within all three of the Abrahamic faiths, i.e. Judaism, Christianity and Islam. In some countries there is a diversity of places of worship to match. However, in some parts one or more groups are denied what they would regard as their ideal place of worship. One example we noted is the Alevi in Turkey (chapter 5) who are challenging the restrictions placed on Cemevis, their own places of worship. The Alevis' distinctiveness is only partly recognised; there is a pluralism deficit.

We should be aware that church architecture and buildings carry great cultural and theological importance for many Christians in the Middle East and are integral to their rites and worship. Church buildings also confer recognition of a place within society and hence contribute to a sense of identity for Christians. An Egyptian Christian leader explained to me, "We exist here because we have a place of worship that has what we consider a significant mark of identification." Such marks include a cross or a domed roof.

Amongst Churches there is variation over the relative significance of architecture and also whether worship is possible without a priest. As a generalisation, for Eastern and Oriental Orthodox Christians the architecture is itself significant and they need an ordained priest to lead worship. Typically, the priest's role is to intone the liturgy; it is the role of monks and bishops to teach the faith. In contrast, architecture is less significant in the Catholic tradition. However, here too a priest is essential to conduct Mass, which is the most meaningful form of service. Within the

Protestant tradition, architecture has little theological significance and many forms of worship can be conducted without an ordained priest, e.g. lay church leader Hamid Pourmand in Iran (chapter 12), although there are exceptions to this general pattern. In all traditions, some locations become special to particular groups of worshippers.

It is not always clear what is Christian tradition, what is individual preference and what is Biblical (in an obvious sense) about church buildings. This can be particularly confusing to converts to Christianity.

Mosques hold a similar significance to some Muslims. They are part of belonging, symbolise a presence, and the height of the minarets are regarded by some as a sign of dominance over the local area. In this context, Egyptian Christians have long complained about the different treatment of mosques and church buildings within the planning regulations. Church leaders long for equal treatment for places of worship.

A related topic is the requirement to be a legally recognised entity in order to own or rent property as well as operate bank accounts, employ staff and sponsor visas for foreign visitors. This applies to religious entities such as churches wishing to operate a building designated as a place of worship. The owners of property designated as a place of worship are typically exempt from property taxes and, in some countries, are provided with free utilities. Turkey is an example. Effectively, this is a state subsidy of religious practice. Such practices increase the desirability of obtaining official recognition of religious bodies. The financial benefits add to the significance of the distinction between being recognised as an "association" or "society" and being recognised as a "religious entity."

Within Christianity there is sometimes a tension between those preferring a building and those with a home based approach to worship services. For those with a religious registration that is not Christian, then the latter might be the only viable option. In some places, what begins as a home based fellowship can expand to the point where operating their own building becomes a viable option. There are a number of factors including affordability of buildings, what best facilitates a sense of belonging, being part of and contributing to a wider community, and what gives those enquiring about Christianity a place to visit and ask questions.

The next stops on our tour of the Middle East are Iraq and Syria. Displacement is all too common, including for Christians. Can the displaced find suitable places to worship in a strange land? For those left behind, travelling to their church can be dangerous. Some have chosen to attend the nearest church building even if it is from a different tradition to that which they attended previously. They were made welcome, with new and long-standing worshippers adapting to the changed dynamic.

One pastor told me that his church was having to make major changes to its services. The congregation was greatly increased as displaced persons attended. Some of these new attendees were not Christian in the religious registration sense. As a pastor, he welcomed them and was pleased to explain the Christian faith to any who wished to learn. Equally, he understood the concerns of many long-standing church members nervous about the presence of a large number of outsiders and fearful of the potential consequences. The displaced were welcome to worship by some, but not by all.

May I worship with you? It is not always clear. For those whose registration does not match the signs on the building, becoming a trusted, accepted and respected member of the community of worshippers can be a long process and some challenges may prove to be insurmountable. Many, however, consider the price worth paying.

Chapter 18

Iraq – a cradle of civilisation

The next country on our regional tour is Iraq. The rivers Euphrates and Tigris flow through Iraq, merging together shortly before flowing into the Gulf. The Gulf is another example in the region of geographic names being problematic. This body of water is referred to by some as the Persian Gulf and by others as the Arabian Gulf. Both names can imply ownership by an ethnic group, which affronts some members of the other ethnicity. The term the Gulf respects this, and reflects that this body of water is a shared resource of all who live around its shores, and of the world as a whole in the international trade that moves across its surface.

The valleys of the major rivers in Iraq have been inhabited for millennia; this area is one of the cradles of human civilisation. It features in religious history as the birthplace of Abraham; Ur of the Chaldeans was located close to the modern city of Basra.

In recent decades, Iraq has been a country involved in a series of conflicts, namely, the Iran-Iraq war (1980-88), the invasion of Kuwait (1990-91) and the 2003 invasion by a US-led coalition that removed Saddam Hussein. The latter led to an insurgency and sectarian violence in parts of the country whose severity has ebbed and flowed ever since. An intense phase began in July 2014 when an armed group seized control of Mosul and other parts of western Iraq and proclaimed itself 'The Islamic State.' It is referred to as ISIS/ISIL[29]

[29] The group's original official title was *The Islamic State of Iraq and ash-Sham*. It is referred to as *The Islamic State in Iraq and Syria* (ISIS)

and Daesh, as we discussed in chapter 13. I will respect the wishes of political leaders in the Middle East and use the term Daesh for this group.

The recent years of conflict have profoundly affected Iraq's multi-religious and multi-ethnic population, amongst whom is a long-established Christian presence. Iraq operates a religious registration system, which has several unique features.

On 25th January 2014 a meeting of the Council of Christian Church Leaders of Iraq was held at the Armenian Orthodox church in Baghdad. The leaders issued a statement expressing the hope that all citizens be granted the right to freely choose their own religious registration when they reached adulthood. This would require new legislation which the church leaders noted must include the civil status of the child with regards to religious matters, including in schools.

How is this call to be understood? Is it asking for the end of religious registration across Iraq or for its amendment to allow change in any direction, as is the

and *The Islamic State in Iraq and the Levant* (ISIL) in some sources. The phrase Belad As-Sham refers to the entire Levant.

case in Lebanon? Is it asking that individuals can choose at age 18? In Jordan, we noted that those whose registration is changed during childhood and adolescence can choose at age 18 whether to take the registration they had at birth or the one to which it has been changed. Is it asking that people can choose on their eighteenth birthday or at any point after they reach 18 years of age? How likely is the call to be implemented?

At present, as in most countries in the Middle East, Christians can change their registration to Muslim but not vice-versa.

The central government maintains what it refers to as three religious endowments, namely the Sunni Endowment, the Shi'a Endowment and the "Christian, Yezidi, Sabean-Mandaean and Other Religions Endowment." These Endowments, operating under the authority of the Prime Minister's office, disburse government funding to maintain and protect religious facilities. The Endowments differentiate between Sunni and Shi'a Muslims. However, Iraqi identity cards state the holder's religion but the options are limited to Muslim, Christian, Yezidi and Mandaean. The small numbers of Baha'i adherents must self-identify themselves as Muslim in order to obtain an identity card. The cards are required to register children in school and to obtain a passport, although passports do not state the holder's religion. The three Endowments are not millets because they do not operate religiously based court systems covering personal status matters.

Prior to 2003, mixed marriages between adherents of Sunni and Shi'a Islam were common in Baghdad. Colloquially, such couples were referred to as "Sushis." Sectarian violence in the years since 2003 has made life difficult for such couples as many were not made welcome in communities that became increasingly homogenised. They chose either to leave Iraq or to move within Iraq, notably to the predominantly Kurdish northern provinces. Some were forced to divorce. The presence of Sushis demonstrates that Muslims were treated as being part of one millet.

The major ethnic groups are Arabs and Kurds, although there are also Turkmen, Shabak and other ethnic groups. Some Arabs and Turkmen are followers of Sunni Islam, others of Shi'a. Almost all Iraqi Kurds are followers of Sunni Islam although there is a small number of Faili Kurds who are Shi'a. The Shabak also follow Shi'a Islam. Ethnically, the population is approximately 75% Arab, 20% Kurd and 5% other. Religiously, Shi'a Islam has the most adherents. Linguistically, the Arabs speak Arabic whilst amongst the Kurds most use either the Sorani or the Bedhini dialects of Kurdish with small numbers using some of the other five Kurdish dialects spoken across the Middle East.

Iraq has developed a complex, multi-tiered governance structure. There is a central government in the capital Baghdad. The country has 18 provinces, each with a provincial governance structure. Three provinces in the north, Arbil, Dahuk and Sulaimaniyah, have formed an autonomous region governed by the Kurdish Regional Government (KRG) with its administrative centre in Arbil.[30]

Since 2005 the central government has comprised a Presidential Council and a parliament. The Presidential Council is composed of a President and two Vice-Presidents with these three people to be a Kurd, a Sunni Arab and a Shi'ite Arab. The council

[30] Arbil is spelt Erbil, and occasionally Irbil, in some sources, with all three spellings being different transliterations of the name into Roman script. Arbil is the form used in official Iraqi sources. The Kurdish name is Hawlêr.

became ineffective in December 2012 when President Talabani (a Kurd) suffered a serious stroke. One year earlier, Tareq al-Hashimi, the Sunni Vice President, fled after being accused by the then Prime Minister Nouri al-Maliki (a Shi'a) of operating death squads. Deputy Prime Minister Saleh Mutlaq (a Sunni) fled at the same time. The Presidential Council's inability to influence events meant that Prime Minister al-Maliki's increasing marginalisation of Sunni communities during 2013 and early 2014 went uncontested. This created the context for Sunni communities to assert control over their own affairs during the summer of 2014. Daesh was one of a number of armed groups involved in these events. Pluralism was significant by its absence in al-Maliki's government.

There is some linkage between religious registration and the political system. Eight of the 325 seats in the Council of Representatives, the parliament, are reserved for members of specific groups. Of these, five are for Christian candidates, one each from the provinces of Baghdad, Ninevah, Kirkuk, Arbil and Dahuk. The other three are one for a Yezidi, one for a Mandaean and one for a Shabak. The KRG likewise reserves seats for designated communities in its parliament; five seats are reserved for Christians, five for Turkmen and one for Armenians. This allocation combines religious terms, i.e. Christian, and ethnic terms, i.e. Turkmen and Armenian. The fact that most Armenians are Christian means that there is potential for duplication in this arrangement.

Iraq has held national and municipal elections since 2005. One observes that many political parties are along ethnic-religious lines. However, some overtly seek to present a broader platform and appeal; they have adopted a pluralist approach. During the municipal elections in Kirkuk in the spring of 2014 one commentator noted that the mayor, ethnically Kurdish, had been re-elected in part due to the votes of non-Kurdish residents pleased that he was exercising his authority for the benefit of all residents of the city. This was noted as remarkable. Kirkuk's population is ethnically diverse, with significant Kurdish, Arabic and Turkmen communities. The city is regarded by many Kurds as historically a Kurdish city. But Saddam Hussein overtly tried to 'Arabise' the city by forcibly displacing Kurds and inducing Arabs to move there from other parts of Iraq.

One senses the desire for change, at least in parts of Iraq, and the frustration at the dysfunctional federal politics. The pluralism deficit has serious consequences across Iraq. Kirkuk's mayoral election suggests that the deficit can be overcome. Proposals made in summer 2015 for changes to the political structure appear motivated at tackling corruption and promoting greater inclusiveness. In the Introduction we asked 'how many Iraqis are there in Iraq?' It would appear that the answer is not enough, although some Iraqis are attempting to improve matters.

The KRG's relationship with the central government is somewhat fractious, and has an effect on the religious registration system. We will summarise the tensions and then explore the relevance to our topic.

One tension is the share of the national budget that is allocated to the KRG. This is a similar discussion to that conducted by many provincial administrations. The absence of a recent census means that an allocation of the national budget to provinces widely endorsed as fair and equitable cannot be achieved. The allocation of parliamentary seats to provinces in 2009 was achieved based on the ration card system, with one seat per 100,000 people. The total number of seats was increased so that more provinces received allocations close to what they expected. Agreement on a census process has proved elusive; representatives of most provinces are reluctant to trust that other areas will not be able to cheat. Corruption is known to be all too common.

Another area of tension between the KRG and the central government is the management and regulation of the oil industry. The KRG would like to pursue rapid development within its area and seeks the financial resource to do so. Consequently, it has signed contracts with multinational companies to increase oil exports. The central government wants to retain control of what it regards as national assets, ensuring that the resulting income is regarded as part of the national budget. However, the central government has failed to enact a hydrocarbons law covering the regulatory framework to be applied. The KRG resents the delays being caused by what it regards as dysfunctional political and administrative decision making in Baghdad. The central government has awarded several new contracts to multinational companies working in southern Iraq, which the KRG regards as the government applying different procedures and methods to various regions within the country.

Another area of concern is the control of heavy weapons. The KRG operates its own security forces, known as Peshmerga, which fulfil a combination of police and military functions. The central government desires that they be equipped only with light arms. The KRG is nervous about the central government's purchase of heavy weapons for the national military forces. It argues that Iraq is very unlikely to need such weapons for use in any conflict with neighbouring states. Therefore the only likely use, other than for national prestige, would be in an internal conflict within Iraq, of which the most likely targets would be the Kurds. The events of summer 2014 when some Iraqi army equipment fell into the hands of Daesh and other armed groups were seen as a fulfilment of such fears. Conversely, the Peshmerga's involvement in confronting Daesh has led to their becoming better equipped.

Finally, there is the matter of the status of Kirkuk. Many Kurds regard this city as historically Kurdish and desire its inclusion within the KRG's region. It is located in the province of the same name and is not part of the KRG's remit. Article 136 of the 2005 Constitution states that a referendum would be held by the end of 2007 to determine whether Kirkuk would become part of the KRG's region. This remains unfulfilled, with no agreement between the authorities in Arbil and Baghdad over the electorate and procedures to be applied. Events of 2014 have had a major effect on this issue too: Peshmerga forces assumed security responsibility for Kirkuk. They are unlikely to relinquish this responsibility.

Having summarised the tensions we now ask the relevance to our topic. The KRG has been asked by several Christians to adjust the religious registration system. One such request in recent years came from a Kurdish Christian who consciously chose not to register the birth of his children because he did not want the word *Muslim* to appear on their birth certificates. His registration is Muslim, and hence the state would register his children as such. When the elder child reached school age, he was not able to enrol the child in any school. The Iraqi identity card is required during the enrolment process and he did not have one for the child because he cannot apply without a birth certificate. Iraqi law requires parents to enrol their children in school before their eighth birthday. Failure to do so leads to the parents losing legal custody of the child who becomes a 'ward of the state.'

The KRG sympathised with his view. However, they responded to his requests by stating that the religious registration system is a national system, and hence comes under the authority of the federal government in Baghdad. We must acknowledge that this is true although we could ask whether there were ways in which they might have been more helpful. It seems clear that the KRG chose not to make this a priority at that time. We can understand their reluctance given their tensions with Baghdad, but it does mean that the identity crisis that they can see for some of their citizens remains unresolved.

Another religious registration matter concerns at least one Christian run orphanage in the KRG area. A few years ago those running an orphanage became aware that some of their children had had their religious registrations changed to Muslim. This raised the problem in some people's eyes of Muslim children being raised by non-Muslim parents/guardians. In most cases, the orphanages became aware of the changes some time after they had been made.

There were three typical scenarios underlying the changed registrations. In some cases a divorced or widowed mother had remarried a Muslim man and the stepfather changed the registration of his step-children. In other cases an estranged father had changed his registration to Muslim in order to marry a lady whose registration is Muslim. The estranged father then changed the children's registration. The third scenario is administrative error. However, correcting this was not practical. Often the children were ethnically Arab and from Mosul and other cities and towns outside the KRG's area having been displaced by sectarian strife. The orphanage leaders were reluctant to travel to such areas to ask for the errors to be corrected. They feared that the local authorities frequently had no process for effecting such changes. Further, some applicants reasoned that areas such as Mosul had, at that time, stricter and more religiously minded judiciaries; consequently, the applicants felt intimidated and lacked confidence that their challenges would be upheld.

There is a similarity here to the reconvert situation in Egypt that we saw in chapter 2. In Egypt, it took a multiyear legal battle to ensure that administrative errors could be corrected at the request of the individuals concerned. In Iraq, the KRG-Baghdad tensions have mitigated against any such process being undertaken.

The current context has deeply affected Iraq's churches. Since 2003 a number of Iraqi Arabs have been internally displaced, including Christians. As we noted for the "Sushis," Christians either emigrated or moved to the KRG's area. The authorities there have allowed recognised Christian churches to operate normally. Mostly they worship in Arabic. The KRG authorities have granted some limited form of recognition to the Kurdish speaking church. In 2004 the Governor of Arbil, with the approval of the KRG's Ministry of Interior, sent a letter to the leaders of a Kurdish church stating that there was no objection to the establishment of this church in Arbil. This has functioned as a registration, although it is not, strictly speaking, a legal registration.

On 4th July 2011 a new Chaldean church building opened in Sikanayan, near Kirkuk. It was the first new building for a recognised church to be opened since 2003.

The Council of Christian Church Leaders of Iraq includes representatives of all 14 officially registered Christian denominations. These include Chaldeans (an eastern rite of the Catholic Church), The Assyrian Church of the East, Syriacs (Eastern Orthodox), Armenian Catholic, Armenian Orthodox (Eastern Orthodox), Anglican and other Protestant denominations. In addition, a number of Protestant denominations operate openly despite not having official recognition. In 2007 one denomination with churches in Baghdad, Basra, Kirkuk and Arbil had an application for official registration rejected by the central government.

The meeting of Church leaders in January 2014 noted at the start of this chapter discussed a second contentious topic, namely unifying the date for the celebration of Easter in all Iraqi churches. The Eastern and Oriental Orthodox churches follow the Julian calendar whereas the Catholic and most Protestant churches use the Gregorian. The date of Easter can be the same, or one week apart or occasionally five weeks apart. The difference affects wider society due to adherents of the different churches desiring a holiday at different times. A unified date would benefit the whole of society.

Here we must leave Iraq and move to the final country on our tour, namely Syria. Here too conflict currently engulfs parts of the country and Christian communities have been displaced from some of their ancestral homes. Iraq was a cradle of human civilisation; hopefully it will become a cradle of pluralistic governance for the benefit of all citizens. Sadly, events since December 2012 have shown what the alternative can look like.

Chapter 19

Syria – a civil war?

Our tour of Middle Eastern countries concludes in Syria. Here, we need to reflect upon how this country was governed prior to 2011 and then add a few brief comments on what remains of this era.

Prior to 2011 Syria operated a religious registration system which was applied across its multi-ethnic and multi-religious society. Religious conversion was not illegal but strongly discouraged. The state officially recognised conversions to Islam but not from it.

Religious registration is stated on birth certificates and restricted to one of Muslim, Christian or Jew. Effectively, there are three millets, with the Muslim one including everyone not accepted as Jewish or Christian. Religious registration is not stated on identity cards, but is required on documentation concerning marriage. Women with registration of Muslim are not allowed to marry non-Muslims, the same restriction that we have seen across the Middle East.

In recent decades the state was religiously tolerant, at least for recognised religious groups working amongst those of the same religious registration. Any element of repression from the government was more political than religious. Likewise, overt proselytising was seen as having a political effect and so was not permitted. There is no law against proselytising, although it was strongly discouraged, primarily for fear that it would cause inter-communal tensions. The question 'May I worship with you?' was emphatically answered by 'yes, provided your registration matches ours.' Religious groups were required to obtain prior approval for all meetings other than advertised worship services. Consequently, church buildings could only be open for advertised services; access for private prayer at other times was not permitted.

Christian and Muslim festivals were recognised as public holidays, namely, Eastern and Western Easters, Christmas Day and the three Muslim festivals of Eid al-Adha, Eid al-Fitr and the Prophet Muhammad's birthday.

The government was very sensitive about ethnic and religious demographics, making accurate figures hard to obtain. One reason for this was that President Basher al-Assad and many other senior government figures were Alawites, a group estimated as being 11% of the population. The Alawites are a religious group that is regarded by some Muslims as a branch of Shi'a Islam. Some Muslims regard the Alawites as heretical and not part of Islam; a number of Alawites agree, regarding their faith as a unique religion. When the Iranian government officially embraced Alawites as part of Shi'a Islam their decision was primarily political – they wanted Syria as an ally.

The Kurdish community was regarded as the largest non-Arab ethnic group in the country. Other ethnic groups include the Turkmen, Cherkess (Adyghe) and Chechen, all of whom, like the vast majority of Kurds, are adherents of Sunni Islam – though their ethnicity is frequently a stronger part of their sense of identity than their religion. There was a very small Jewish community.

Most of Syria's Christians lived in Damascus or Aleppo, with significant groups elsewhere including Homs. It is commonly reported that 10% of Syrians are Christians, but this is a long-standing estimate which, in the absence of clear demographic data, is open to question. In 2012 a study from Aleppo suggested that the figure may be far lower.[31]

Numerically, the largest Christian church is the Byzantine/Greek Orthodox Church under the Patriarchate of Antioch and All the East based in Damascus. There are fully recognised churches belonging to the Catholic, the Eastern Orthodox (to which the Greek Orthodox church belongs), the Oriental Orthodox and the Protestant families of churches, plus the Assyrian Church of the East which does not belong to any of these groups.

Other religious groups are the Druze, Yezidis, Arab-Shi'a and Ismailis, all of which are numerically smaller than the Christian community. The personal status matters of all these groups are handled within the Muslim millet. The Kurds and several other communities have their own languages. None have official recognition and so cannot be used for official purposes. Amongst Christians, this is also true for the Syriac and Assyrian communities.

[31] Joshua Landis; 18th February 2012;
http://www.joshualandis.com/blog/the-poor-plight-of-the-christian-minority-in-aleppo-syria-by-ehsani (accessed 20th February 2014)

The situation in Syria changed in 2011; the Arab Awakening profoundly affected Syria. When it began, some had a positive expectation that change could and would be well managed; others feared that it would unleash pent up anger to which the government would respond harshly.

Syria had been affected by a serious drought beginning in 2009. Many agricultural areas were devastated and many migrated to the cities looking for alternative work.[32] The government's response was minimal; one can debate whether this was due to callous neglect or genuine lack of government resources. The effect was to create a large number of unemployed and disaffected people; protesters' calls for more and better jobs were particularly poignant in Syria.

Armed conflict arose in Syria during 2011. Demonstrations occurred in several towns and cities, including Damascus, Aleppo, Homs, Hama, Latakia, Dera'a and Baniyas. There were pro as well as anti-government demonstrations. President Assad

---

[32] One source estimated that one million people migrated to cities. Accurate figures are not available but what is clear is that the number of people affected was considerable.

promised reforms and on 19th April he rescinded the State Emergency Legislation that had operated since 8th March 1963, i.e. six years before his father Hafez al-Assad seized power in a coup. Under these laws, suspects could be detained without charge or trial, trials could be conducted without due process (e.g. civilians tried before military tribunals), freedom of expression was curtailed, and communications were monitored. It is worth keeping in mind that Syria has known periods of internal conflict in most decades since the modern state was formed in 1946. Hafez Assad brought 'peace' – in the sense of the absence of conflict – but at a price.

However, the peaceful demonstrations continued due to the limited nature of the response to protesters' demands. The middle classes in the largest city, Aleppo, as well as in Damascus had remained largely quiet; only in Homs had demonstrators convincingly bridged social and communal divides. Some ethnic-religious groups either openly sided with the government (including in some Christian areas), or kept a relatively low profile (e.g. in the Kurdish-dominated northeast and the Druze town of Suweida), or were crushed into submission by government forces (e.g. in the Ismaili town of Salamiya).

On 23rd December 2011 there were coordinated twin car bombings in Damascus. This development marked a change in the pattern of violence. The government blamed an al-Qaeda affiliated group – the attack fitted the common al-Qaeda practice of coordinated attacks. During 2012 armed clashes spread to major cities including Homs, Hama, Damascus and Aleppo with the government using aerial bombing of areas controlled by opposition groups, including suburbs of major cities. At the end of 2012 many areas were under the effective control of armed groups, tribal elders or ethnic groups. Notable among the latter were the predominantly Kurdish areas in the north east. This situation has continued, with constant, slow changes in who-controls-where due to clashes amongst: (a) the government and groups loyal to it; (b) the numerous armed groups opposed to the government, who sometimes fight amongst themselves; and (c) Kurdish and other groups seeking to maintain cohesive administration of their communities.

The Christian community has been affected by the conflict in several ways. Christians were forced to choose whether to support the government, support the opposition or attempt to remain neutral (with the risk of being attacked by either side). Other groups within society faced the same dilemma, although it was particularly intense for Christians who were frequently perceived as being in favour of the status-quo under President Assad. It must be noted that the vast majority of Christians did still genuinely side with the Assad-led government, without condoning in any way the violence or other abuses perpetrated by government personnel prior to and during the crisis. Christians acknowledge that President Assad is from a similarly-sized religious group (at least according to the commonly accepted demographic) and has allowed the church to operate within Christian communities. Many Christians feared the imposition of an Islamist government which might be installed were the current government to be removed.

In August 2011 General Daoud Rajha, a Christian, was appointed Minister of Defence. (The previous incumbent had stepped down due to serious ill health.) This was the first time the post had been held by a Christian. Some Church leaders were concerned that his appointment would lead to a backlash against Christians because military aspects of the crackdown on protests were being led by a Christian. General Rajha was assassinated on 18th July 2012 in an attack on the National Security Offices in Damascus.

There were violent attacks on some Christian neighbourhoods or communities and some church property. Consequently, Christians were forced to choose whether to remain where they were, relocate within the country or attempt to leave. During 2012 there was a subtle shift in how Syrian church leaders typically interpreted events. Claims of the deliberate targeting of Christians for religious reasons increased as the year progressed. Initially, most were careful to stress that there was little religious targeting, but almost all church leaders seemed fearful of the growing extremist elements within the opposition movement, e.g. Jabhat al-Nusra (see Glossary) and the group that became known as Daesh (whom we met in Iraq).

Finally, there were kidnapping attacks, many for ransom, with some specifically targeting Christian leaders. One high profile case began on 22nd April 2013 when two bishops based in Aleppo, Yohanna Ibrahim of the Syriac Orthodox Church and Boulos Yaziji of the Greek Orthodox Church, were kidnapped when returning to Aleppo from an area close to the border with Turkey. At the time of writing, their whereabouts and fate are unknown.

Official casualty figures for the Syrian crisis have been issued by the United Nations on several occasions. On 25th July 2013 Ban Ki-moon, General Secretary of the UN, solemnly announced that these figures had passed the 100,000 mark. These only include deaths that have been properly recorded, meaning they ignore those whose deaths have gone unreported and whose bodies have been, at best, buried informally. They also exclude those who die due to the absence of medical care or regular medication. Some estimates say that the latter category is probably larger than the actual combat deaths. The human cost of the Syrian crisis is huge.

Syrian Christian leaders have asked me not to describe the Syrian crisis as a "civil war." Their view is based on the number of foreign fighters actively participating with the government and the numerous groups opposed to it, as well as the clear support of numerous other countries for the different parties to the crisis. It used to be said that Lebanon was where regional and international powers fought their battles using someone else's territory. In this regard, Syria has replaced Lebanon.

Life continues in those parts of Syria under stable local governance. Births, marriages and burials continue; the religious registration system remains operative. Some church buildings are open at times other than those of advertised services. Such buildings have become centres of care for the needy.

Syria completes our tour of the Middle East, but not of the Arab world. We will take a look at North Africa and then the Arabian Peninsula, the original home of the Arab peoples. Before that, Syria prompts a pause to reflect on the term "martyrdom," the ultimate cost of being faithful to one's religious beliefs and convictions.

Chapter 20

Who is a Martyr?

This question has significance within both Christianity and Islam. Relevant to our focus of religious registration is the extent to which people are willing to be identified as adherents of a particular faith, or group within a faith, when to do so exposes them to religiously motivated violence or other risks.

We will look at martyrdom within Islam sandwiched between considerations of martyrdom within Christianity. There are a variety of approaches in both faiths.

During 2014 there was discussion about how many Christians were being killed worldwide because of their religious beliefs, with widely differing numbers being stated by different sources. As with all statistics, the definitions used are crucial, as are the methods used for performing the necessary counts.

The word martyr derives from the Greek word for witness, i.e. a martyr is a witness. The broadest definition of martyrdom used by some is "those killed by human hostility due to their witness." Consequently this includes those who remain in places of conflict in order to maintain faithful witness to their faith, even if their subsequent death is due to inter-tribal violence or (so called) 'collateral damage.' Under this broad definition, analysis by several groups gave an estimated 100,000 martyrdoms of Christians worldwide during 2013. Precise numbers are not available as the majority of the deaths occur in conflict zones, with consequent minimal formality in record keeping. This figure of 100,000 during 2013 was regarded as typical for most years.

In the Syrian crisis it has been noted that deaths due to degraded medical care and food supplies probably exceed deaths due to the direct effects of armed conflict. Those who remain in areas with humanitarian needs expose themselves to risks to their own health, wellbeing and even life. Under the broadest interpretation, these people are also martyrs; they are the indirect victims of human hostility and the denial of humanitarian aid as a weapon of war.

A narrower definition used by some is to count deaths in which Christians are specifically killed because of their faith or Christian activities, and limit the counting to formally recorded deaths. This narrower definition was used in the compilation of the World

Watch List issued by Open Doors in January each year. According to their analysis, 2,123 Christians were martyred in the 12 month period 1st November 2012 to 31st October 2013. The majority of cases were in Syria and Nigeria with 1,213 and 612 respectively, followed by Pakistan (88) and Egypt (83).[33] These numbers are questioned by some commentators, as the actual motivation is often hard to determine, with elements of inter-tribal conflict and economic advantage involved in addition to religious considerations.

One example from Syria occurred on 7th April 2014 when Father Frans van der Lugt, a 75 year-old Dutch priest who had been resident in Syria for more than 40 years, was murdered in the Bustan ad-Diwan neighbourhood of Homs. Father van der Lugt was killed by an assailant who entered his residence, took him outside and shot him. He had remained in Syria despite the known risks in order to maintain his Christian witness. Talal al-Barazi, then governor of Homs province, claimed that the perpetrator was associated with Jabhat al-Nusra, an al-Qaeda affiliated

---

[33] Published by World Watch Monitor, 8th January 2014; https://www.worldwatchmonitor.org/2014/01/2935607/ (accessed 29th July 2015)

group in control of that area. Father ven der Lugt is a martyr under both definitions.

In contrast, the deaths on 12th April 2014 of two Armenian Christians in Aleppo killed during shelling are martyrdoms under the broad definition but not the narrower one. There is no evidence to suggest that this was other than 'collateral damage' in a conflict zone.

We noted when considering the Arab Awakening the desire of Christians in the Middle East to maintain faithful witness to Christ. Iraqi and Syrian church leaders strongly desire that Iraqi and Syrian Christians remain in the region and do not seek emigration outside the Middle East. As pastors, they are well aware of the traumas that many have been through and understand why some choose to leave, or seek to do so.

Within Islam, martyrdom is debated and differing opinions exist, notably on suicide bombing. Within most Islamic discourse, a martyr is a warrior who willingly fights for an Islamic cause and trusts his God as to whether or not he lives or dies during combat. Taking one's own life, i.e. suicide, is almost universally condemned within Islam. Those who commit suicide are guaranteed not to be accepted into heaven, in contrast with those killed as warriors who are assured of entry to heaven. This makes the concept of suicide bombing controversial. Such a person has assumed for themselves the decision of whether they live or die during conflict; some argue that this is committing suicide, and hence forbidden; others that it is dying in conflict. This is literally life or death in the eternal, religious sense.

Let me conclude this chapter by returning to Christianity. A few years ago a number of Christians in the Middle East were killed while proselytising in a neighbouring country. The group they were with was travelling to villages and small towns to show a film about the life of Jesus. The group was ambushed; some were killed, others wounded. A few months later the organiser was asked how he and his organisation responded to such an incident. "We train another team and send them." The Westerner who asked was somewhat surprised at such a matter-of-fact reply. The organiser continued, "the trouble with Westerners is that you expect to live; we who live here know that some people will die; for us, conflict is normal." Such an attitude embraces being identified as a Christian, and one who is committed to enabling non-Christians to hear the message of Jesus and have the opportunity to choose to become one of His followers; it accepts risks for the sake of overt witness.

This attitude is not universal within the church in the Middle East. Some church leaders adopt more cautious approaches which we might term as being pastorally focussed on those whose religious registration is Christian. They devote themselves to the task of caring for, serving and teaching Christians. They avoid activities amongst those not registered as Christians to minimise the chances of conflict affecting the community that they serve. Religious registration has a role in risk management.

There are risks in overt proselytising, both for the participants and the Christian communities of which they are a part. We have noted at several points the risks for those who choose to become Christians; for apostates (see chapter 13), identifying with Christ is innately risky. One example of Christians being told that they should be killed for apostasy is recorded in Maryam Rostampour and Marziyeh Amirizadeh's book *Captive in Iran*. A number of fellow detainees responded to being told why these two Christians were being detained by stating that they should be killed. The attitude of most towards these two ladies changed as people got to know them.[34] There are reports of Christians being murdered because of their apostasy from several countries in the region. Most are hard to verify and in my opinion the iceberg metaphor is appropriate, i.e. we observe a small fraction of this challenge; it is unknown how many such Christians are discreetly killed by relatives, with females in particular at risk of becoming victims of (so called) honour killings. In cases with a religious motivation it is likely that the perpetrators would be able to act with impunity.

One high profile murder of Christians from a Muslim background occurred on 18th April 2007 in Malatya, Turkey. Two Turkish Christians, Necati Aydin and Uğur Yuksel, apostates, together with a German Christian, Tilmann Geske, were murdered at the Zirve Publishing House where they worked. Five men were arrested at the scene and charged with the murders. Subsequently others were arrested and charged in connection with the murders. At the time of writing their trial remained on-going, reflecting the

---

[34] Rostampour & Amirizadeh; Captive in Iran; (Tyndale, 2013) e.g. page 107

complexity of the factors and motivations behind this criminal act. Of note for our topic are the pluralism deficit in Turkey, both ethnically and religiously, and the teaching of religious intolerance within the education system that we noted in chapter 5.[35] There are often multiple factors at work in religiously motivated crimes.

In 2007 Jordan initiated a programme to address honour crimes together with domestic violence. Queen Rania participated in the launch and has continued to be involved in public awareness aspects of the programme. Some legal changes have been made, such as increasing prison sentences, and proposed, such as stating that the defence of acting whilst in a rage is inadmissible. It is worth noting that justice can be administered by law in honour-shame cultures and that greater respect for diversity would contribute to it becoming the accepted norm. It is one way to address the pluralism deficit.

[35] See James Wright; *The Martyrs of Malatya;* (EP Books, 2015) pages 130, 184 and 189-193

Chapter 21

North Africa – a cradle of Christian theology

We return to our tour of the region. Having looked at each country in the Middle East, we will summarise the situations in North Africa and the Arabian Peninsula. In these areas, the concept of religious registration is applied in a different way.

North Africa features heavily in early Church history, with early Christian theologians and church leaders such as Tertullian and Augustine coming from this area. Christian theology was shaped in these lands. This changed in the seventh century with the emergence of Arab empires and the spread of Islam across North Africa. The governments of Mauritania, Morocco, Algeria, Tunisia and Libya regard their citizens as Muslims, with only a few exceptions. Algeria and Morocco make due allowance for their small Jewish communities.

The concepts of religious registration underlie this situation. Morocco can be regarded as having 'one millet plus an appendage,' with the appendage covering a distinct and small ethnic-religious community, i.e. the Jewish community. Libya, Mauritania and Tunisia are less clear about the appendage, while the situation in Algeria is more complex. The consequence is that all personal status matters are handled using Islamic rites and applying Islamic principles except for the due allowance being made for the Jewish communities.

The recognition of Jewish communities is our first glimpse into the ethnic mix of these countries. There are Arab peoples here. Libya, Tunisia, Algeria and Morocco all have Berber peoples, with 'Berber' being a generic term for numerous distinct tribal groups resident in these areas prior to the spread of the Arab empire along the Mediterranean coast in the seventh century. Mauritania is more diverse because it is where North Africa meets Sub-Saharan Africa.

The effects on the daily lives of those who have chosen to become Christians are often profound, notably for families with children. At home, the children are raised as Christian, yet at school they are told they are Muslim. As one Christian told me, "This is deeply confusing to their young minds. However, my wife and I need to bring them up knowing how to live as Christians in a Muslim majority country. So they do need to understand Islam, not as adherents but as fellow citizens with many who are Muslim."

Another North African Christian remarked that, "I am a follower of Jesus, which makes me a Christian. Yet my country, my government and my society, treats me as though I am a Muslim. The government refuses to recognise or acknowledge my decision to follow Jesus. There is no mechanism by which the change can be recognised because the government has refused to create such a mechanism. Indeed, society refuses to accept that such a change is possible, despite the testimony of people like me who have embraced Christianity."

There are some variations amongst these countries. We will focus on Algeria, but first a brief comment on Tunisia, where there are some provisions within the state education system. There is a long-standing but little known law that allows parents to instruct schools to withdraw their children from religious education classes. All state schools teach Islam. Most indigenous Christians choose not to exercise their rights under the law, mostly so as not to isolate their children from friends and neighbours, and draw unnecessary attention to their choice of faith.

We noted in chapter 10 that Tunisia is where the Arab Awakening erupted. It is worth noting that prior to 2011 Tunisia was regarded by expatriate Christians as, in general, a friendly and relaxed country in which to live. In many areas, notably in education and women's employment, Tunisia had made remarkable progress, although less progress had been made in the area of political freedom where state control had been maintained. Like other Arab countries, Tunisia was aware that there was an Islamist extremist element within society. Most human rights problems reported concerning Tunisia were related to this. Consequently, it entered the new era heralded by the Arab Awakening from a position of strength in some areas. At the time of writing Tunisia appears to be handling the transition of its political system with greater dexterity and sense of national cohesion than other countries, notably its neighbour Libya. The extremist element was apparent in 2013 when two political assassinations occurred[36] and in 2015 when high-profile attacks on tourists occurred in March and June.

---

[36] Namely, Chokri Belaid, a prominent member of the opposition, on 6th February and Mohamed Brahmi, leader of the Movement of the People party, on 25th July.

Now for Algeria, which has allowed some formal legal recognition of indigenous churches whose members are all from Muslim backgrounds. The only other area where this is true in the Middle East and North Africa is the Kurdish Regional Government area of northern Iraq. In Algeria, the government is telling Christians that they are Muslims and giving them some recognition as churches! Religious registration is not about belief and practice; the government's position is inconsistent.

Back in the 1970s the Algerian government approached the Protestant churches to articulate a problem. When the government wished to communicate with the Catholic and Orthodox churches they knew whom to approach, namely their presiding bishops, but there was no equivalent single point of contact for the various Protestant churches. The leaders of the Protestant churches responded by establishing the L'Église Protestante d'Algerie, or EPA for short, literally 'The Protestant Church of Algeria.' This body was granted official recognition by the government.

It should be noted that the EPA is an association, not a denomination, enabling individual churches to retain their own character. When formed in the 1970s, the membership was exclusively churches serving expatriate Christians. However, the situation in Algeria has changed; the twenty-first century is different from the twentieth both in the religious demographic and the legal framework for non-Muslim worship.

The religious demographic started to change when many expatriates left the country as civil unrest erupted in the 1990s. It is generally estimated that 150,000 people were killed. Many others were internally displaced with estimates for 1992 ranging from 500,000 to as many as 1.5 million people (4-5% of the population). Many relocated to the outskirts of large urban areas, creating slum areas with high unemployment, poverty and some malnutrition. The government continues to strive to respond adequately. It is understood that many have been able to return, although no survey has been undertaken in recent years.

During this period, and continuing since, there has been the emergence of indigenous churches serving Algerians who have chosen to become Christians.

There have been several changes in the law. A change in the Law of Associations required all associations to re-register. The EPA duly submitted its application to re-register in 2005. They did not receive a reply. In early 2011 the EPA made a submission direct to parliament in order to avoid the Ministry of Religious Affairs and to make their application more public. In July 2011 their registration application was approved.

On 12th January 2013 it became clear that the EPA's status was under renewed threat. New legislation concerning the regulations governing associations included the requirement that each association must have representation in at least 12 of Algeria's 48 provinces. At that time, the EPA was only represented in five provinces. During 2013 the EPA was able to accept into its membership churches in seven additional provinces, thereby successfully meeting the new minimum requirement.

One challenge was resolved, but another remains ongoing. This concerns the EPA's member churches' difficulties in registering their buildings as places of worship. They desired to meet their legal requirements but poor administration was preventing them from doing so.

In 2006 the government published Ordinance 06-03 concerning non-Muslim religious groups. This legislation requires all such religious groups to officially register, and that all worship services must be held in places dedicated for religious use and such places must be registered with the state. Religious entities violating the law can be fined and have their assets, including their buildings, confiscated. These requirements meant that Algerian Christians were dependent on local officials fulfilling their responsibilities quickly, accurately and in an unbiased manner. Registration of churches proved problematic because neither the Ministry of Interior nor the Ministry of Justice accepted responsibility for overseeing the process.

This prompted the issuing of Executive Decree 07-158 to establish the administrative body described by the legislation, namely The National Commission for Non-Muslim Religious Services (NCNMR). This was to be presided over by the Minister of Religious Affairs and Awqaf (Religious Endowments), and comprise senior representatives of the Ministries of Defence, Interior, Foreign Affairs and National Security, as well as the National Police Headquarters and the quasi-governmental National Consultative Commission for the Promotion and Protection of Human Rights. The NCNMR held its first meeting in 2008, although at the start of 2014 it had not established an administrative means for non-Muslim religious groups to register with the government. Christians seeking to comply with the law have been prevented from doing so.

In contrast, the government has approved the reopening of 25 synagogues. They are the only non-Muslim community to have had any applications made under Ordinance 06-03 accepted. One suspects that the reason is that the Jewish community, while defined ethnically, is recognised as also distinct religiously. There is no element of conversion here; born a Jew and will therefore remain Jewish. We can also note that it is another example of the law being applied inequitably to all in a religious matter.

Another aspect of Ordinance 06-03 is that it forbids proselytising Muslims. A number of people have been prosecuted under this law. Each has used the defence that they simply responded to questions they were asked and to polite requests to give someone a Bible or New Testament.

A problem with the legislation is that it does not define proselytising. In Algeria, and at least one other North African country, the phrase 'shaking the faith of a Muslim' has been used during court hearings in such cases. The phrase 'shaking the faith' reflects the government's treatment of all citizens as Muslims. That is what they were at birth and it is how they will always be regarded. Belief, practice or individual choice are immaterial. The concept that a Muslim can convert to another faith does not exist. We might say that one cannot be an apostate! Therefore, proselytising cannot be defined as inviting someone to convert to another religion. So, proselytising is reduced to being about asking someone to consider another religion, with consequent reflection on their own. Hence the expression of 'shaking the faith of a Muslim.'

Two other aspects of Ordinance 06-03 are worth mentioning here. Both concern acts of worship. The legislation mandates that such acts, i.e. services, be conducted in a place designated as exclusively for religious practice. Effectively, this criminalises house fellowship meetings. Further, Executive Decree 07-135 specified that religious events need to be approved by the *wali* (i.e. governor equivalent) at least five days before the event. Does this mean all regular services, or is the scope limited to special events?

The Algerian government states that all citizens are Muslims yet gives legal recognition to indigenous Christians. Underlying this apparent contradiction is the concept of being born into a religious community and the absence of respecting individual choice of religious belief and practice – a pluralism deficit.

Chapter 22

Arabian Peninsula – cradle of the Arabs and Islam

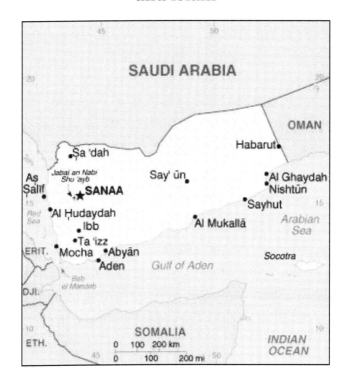

We complete our tour of the region with a visit to the Arabian Peninsula. This is the original home of the Arabs, who spread more widely in the seventh and eighth centuries.

As with the North African countries, the seven countries of the Arabian Peninsula – Bahrain, Kuwait, Oman, Qatar, Saudi Arabia, United Arab Emirates and Yemen – regard almost all citizens as Muslims. The exceptions are in Yemen, which makes due allowance for its small Jewish community, and Bahrain and Kuwait, which make some provision for their small indigenous Christian communities. Both these Christian communities are descendants of Arab Christians in the Levant (literally, the lands around Damascus) who were resident in Bahrain and Kuwait when the states were formed in 1971 and 1961 respectively.

There are large numbers of expatriate Christians within six of these countries resident as migrant workers and as students. The exception is Yemen, which is a much poorer country than the others. In five countries the expatriates are served by a variety of churches, mostly operating on compounds which comprise places of worship for Eastern Orthodox, Oriental Orthodox, Catholic and Protestant churches meeting in distinct buildings located within an officially recognised site. These churches use a wide variety of languages, allowing many migrants to worship in their mother tongue. This includes a number of Arabic speaking groups, attended by Christians from Egypt, Iraq, Jordan, Lebanon, Syria and elsewhere. The exception is Saudi Arabia, which does not permit places of worship for any non-Muslim religion.

A few Arab Christians from Muslim backgrounds have sought jobs in the Arabian Peninsula where they often have greater freedom to attend Arabic speaking churches than in their own countries. The religious registration of attendees is not checked. So, 'may I worship with you?' is answered with 'yes, come on in!' Also relevant is that the cultural differences between Muslim and Christian communities seen in many Middle Eastern countries are less apparent when members of those communities are living as migrants in another country. The shared nationality becomes a stronger bond when outside one's country of origin.

Some indigenous Christians experience challenges concerning their religious status. One illustration occurred a few years ago when a lady wished to marry an Indian Christian living and working in her country. The problem was that the lady's father was Muslim, although her mother was an expatriate Christian who was regarded as Muslim in the religious registration sense following her marriage to a national. Consequently, the government considered the lady to be a Muslim, and hence a marriage to a non-Muslim would be illegal.

The lady made indirect enquiries with the Interior Ministry about changing her religious registration to Christian. She received a strong message that such an application was extremely unlikely to succeed and could prove dangerous for her. So she decided not to pursue the matter. This lady tried a discreet enquiry first before considering whether or not to take the risks and costs associated with a legal (and public) challenge. This is a different approach to that which Mohammed Hegazy adopted in Egypt (see chapter 2); he went directly for an overt, highly public legal challenge.

This left the only legal option for the lady and her fiancé for him to officially convert to Islam. Following a civil marriage conducted under an Islamic rite, a church wedding was conducted, despite some initial threats by her family. The threats added a family dimension to the legal injustice elements of their situation.

The couple were only too aware that any children born to them might face the same dilemma. We need to note that another issue in many Arab countries is that citizenship follows the father; consequently, this couple's children might struggle to obtain citizenship in the Arabian Peninsula. If they were to obtain such citizenship, then the ramifications of religious registration would continue into the next generation.

During our regional tour we have noted several instances of where the clear rule of law has not been applied equally to all. Saudi Arabia is an interesting illustration of how this can arise.

Most Saudi legislation takes the form of a recommended interpretation of Shari'a law to be applied by the various courts. Many aspects of law remain largely un-codified. That sounds fine, until we realise that there is no coordinated interpretation and administration of Shari'a law at local levels. (In Iran we noted that the legal system stipulated consulting the Supreme Leader's office to ensure consistency of application of Shari'a in situations where there was no codified law.) This leads to inconsistency within the judicial system from one area to another, and in the same area whenever judges change jobs. A further variation is that there are often four different punishments for the same crime depending on whether the perpetrator(s) and victim(s) are Muslim or non-Muslim, and if Muslims, which Medhab, i.e. tradition of Islamic legal jurisprudence, the perpetrator(s) follow.

The business community in particular find this situation profoundly unhelpful. The government is responding with a programme of codifying the law and a training programme for judges. The desire for economic development to provide more jobs is one motivation for the government's actions. The Arab Awakening theme of more and better jobs is prompting transformation of the country's legal system – or at least part thereof.

The lack of consistency in the application of the 'law' affects expatriate Christians living in the country. In 2009, the Vice President of the National Human Rights Commission stated that "the Kingdom does not restrict non-Muslims to practise their religion in private." He told the UN Human Rights Council that, although as the cradle of Islam Saudi Arabia cannot formally host churches, non-Muslims in Saudi Arabia enjoy freedom of worship "and can practise the rituals of their religions in their own places." The policy has been restated at length since 2009.

In practice, there remains a lack of clarity because the law is not formally codified and so is open to interpretation. Nowhere is it clarified if "private" means a nuclear family meeting in their own home, or a small gathering of friends in a private home, or with neighbours. This results in differing practices due to different interpretation by local officials, or even in the same location if officials change. This causes confusion and can lead to people being arrested for what they have been told by others is acceptable.

A number of Saudi Arabian citizens are seeking to be recognised as atheists. During 2013, some met physically, and there were online meetings and discussions. Religious registration is not about belief and practice; likewise a constitutional assertion that all citizens are Muslim says nothing about people's beliefs and practices.

We will conclude our time in the Arabian Peninsula with a brief look at Yemen. Yemen is a complex and diverse country with a turbulent past, and one where the Arab Awakening has contributed to a new phase of conflict and to an initiative that addresses the pluralism deficit – the latter being our focus here.

Yemen, like Sudan, is a highly tribal society. It is also religiously diverse although predominantly Muslim. There are adherents of several strands of both Shi'a and Sunni Islam. One long-standing factor underlying conflict has been the over allocation of national resources to the capital, Sana'a, to the detriment of the provinces, a similar issue to that which we saw in Sudan.

Protests erupted in early 2011, with both pro- as well as anti-government demonstrations in Sana'a and other cities. Some protests became violent, especially in the Sana'a area where heavy weapons were used. President Saleh formerly stood down in February 2012, replaced as President by Abdurabu Mansour Hadi, his long-standing deputy, who was granted a two-year transitional term of office by the Parliament. A National Dialogue process took place from March 2013 to January 2014 involving tribal elders and representatives drawn from across society including women, youth and groups seeking independence for the southern part of the country. The National Dialogue process recommended the adoption of a federal structure with six regions and made proposals for a civil state that respected human rights, strengthened judicial independence, advanced the participation of women in government, and provided universal education and health care. These proposals fulfil many of the aspirations of the Arab Awakening and address the pluralism deficit – or they would do so if they were implemented.

Alas, the government in Sana'a failed to implement the proposals, with factionalism amongst major players being one impediment. They were not helped by some groups stating their rejection of the recommendations, notably al-Hiraak al-Janoubi (Southern Movement) which continued calling for independence for southern provinces.

In September 2014 an armed group, Ansar Allah, forcibly took control of Sana'a and in January 2015 forced the President and Prime Minister to leave office. Ansar Allah's members are predominantly from the Houthi ethnic group whose traditional territory is in the northwest and who are adherents of Zaidism, a strand within Shi'a Islam. It is an organisation with political, social and armed wings. Of note is that the group stated their intention to form an inclusive government and invited others to participate with the stipulation that any ideology that rejected those who were ethnically or religiously different must be discarded. This directly challenges the pluralism deficit.

Other parties declined the invitation to form an inclusive government, resulting in a lack of a broadly accepted effective governance. On 20th February 2015 UN mediated talks resulted in agreement on a five-member Presidential Council, the continuance of the Parliament and the formation of a Transitional Council with a membership similar to that of the National Dialogue to replace the former upper house of parliament. Alas, these arrangements were not given the opportunity to provide effective, inclusive governance as further conflict erupted and other countries became involved militarily. At the time of writing conflict continued, with a plethora of armed groups involved, some of which were being overtly supported by the military forces of other countries.

Ansar Allah have striven for autonomy for many years and what is known as the Sixth Houthi war against the government ended in February 2010. During 2011 they reasserted control of Saada Province and during 2012 took control of al-Jawf province and parts of Hajja province. Their expansion continued during 2013 and during 2014 they exploited factional infighting in Sana'a to expand their influence into that city. They are understood to have been assisted by the tribe and political party of former President Saleh who sought to reduce the influence of the tribe and political party of his successor, President Hadi.[37] So Ansar Allah were now working with a group that they had been in conflict with during 2010.

The National Dialogue process utilised broad-based, pluralistic discussions. Subsequent events have shown the strength of factional infighting and the prevalence of many to work for the exclusive benefit of their own communities rather than a broader common good. Addressing the pluralism deficit will take time.

Our tour of the region draws to an end. In the next chapter we will look at the subject of burial, a challenge that is seen across North Africa and the Arabian Peninsula with some profound implications for Christians. Following this we will look at how what we have seen on our tour compares with international norms before summarising our findings from a

[37] One source here is Sada Journal, 18th September 2014, http://carnegieendowment.org/sada/2014/09/18/saleh-bites-back/hpc0 (accessed 19th February 2015)

variety of perspectives. *"Help us find a way through"* – we are almost in a position to do so.

Chapter 23

Where will I be buried?

We have noted that a number of countries in North Africa and the Arabian Peninsula regard all citizens as Muslims. This has prompted a number of citizens to ask, "If I became a Christian, where would I be buried?" In some of these countries, there are a few cemeteries for expatriate Christians but there are none for nationals. I heard once of a Westerner considering seeking funds to purchase land and establish Christian cemeteries in order that people's choice of faith might be respected at the time of their burial. He chose not to proceed with such a project, reasoning that such a cause would be difficult to promote in the West and, more importantly, would draw attention to the national Christians that they did not want. (The reader will note that the country is not named here for the same reason.)

A related issue is burial sites for expatriates in those states with large numbers of migrant workers. That deaths will occur amongst members of such communities is inevitable given the number of those working in the vibrant economies of Qatar and other Gulf States. Cremation is not permitted in several countries because it is not allowed by Islam. It is the preferred rite for some Asian religions. Consequently, such people must have their bodies repatriated, which is expensive, in order for their requests to be fulfilled.

In several countries it is problematic to find suitable places for the burial of expatriate Christians who die while working in the region. For example, among the sizeable Ethiopian communities resident in Yemen the Ethiopian church is denied freedom to bury their dead using Christian rites. A small number have been transported to Aden and buried at the Anglican cemetery, while others are repatriated to Ethiopia if their families can afford it.

During the Turkey leg of our regional tour we noted two examples of people being buried in Muslim cemeteries despite being Christians. In one case, the person concerned, Uğur, had been murdered because of his Christian activities; yet even in these tragic circumstances he was buried using Islamic burial rites.

While we were considering Iran we noted the increasing lack of respect for indigenous Christian communities and Christian heritage. This lack of respect includes cemeteries. In February 2012 it was reported that a cemetery in Bushehr, used by expatriate and then Armenian Christian communities for more than a century, had been desecrated after falling into disrepair. During 2013 the licence for Tehran's largest Christian cemetery, located in Darvazeh Doulab, was revoked by the authorities.

Places of burial play a significant role in one other aspect of religious identification. In Israel we noted the requirement for those wishing to emigrate to Israel to demonstrate their Jewish ancestry. One method commonly used is to present certificates showing that a grandmother or great grandmother was buried in a Jewish cemetery, thereby demonstrating that that relative was accepted as part of the Jewish community.

Chapter 24

Universal Declaration, Universal Rights

We have completed our survey of the region noting how religious registration is applied. We now look at the international understanding of religious freedom within the broader context of the modern understanding of human rights.

The concept of human rights dates back throughout much of human history. We can point to the Hammurabi Code and the Ten Commandments as early examples of succinct summaries of the rights and duties of each member of a community. Most human societies have a sense of the responsibilities, duties and privileges of their members, and some understanding of the balance amongst individuals, nuclear families, extended families and wider communities.

Magna Carta, signed on 15th June 1215, was a significant document in the establishment of the principle of the rule of law applied equally to all. In Latin, it addressed the question of 'Rex Lex or Lex Rex?' Here Rex means king or ruler and Lex means law. Is the King the law, able to do whatever he chooses with complete impunity, or is the law supreme and even the monarch is subject to it? Magna Carta was a significant development in the historical process of ending arbitrary, authoritarian rule in favour of the rule of law. In many parts of the Middle East, and elsewhere, arbitrary rule continues. During our regional tour, we noted inconsistent application of law in Jordan, Egypt and Saudi Arabia.

The foundation of the modern concept of human rights can be dated to the Universal Declaration of Human Rights adopted by the United Nations' General Assembly on 10th December 1948.

The United Nations was established in October 1945 and its Charter, to which all member states subscribe, includes the protection of human rights. However, the Charter does not define what those rights are. The need for a document to provide a succinct summary was evident to all. The idea of a Universal Declaration was born.

There were two components to the declaration's drafting process. In January 1947 a commission was formed with broad representation and chaired by Eleanor Roosevelt, wife of US President Theodore Roosevelt. Her presence brought considerable stature, attention and kudos to the process. The commission sent questionnaires to numerous individuals and groups worldwide, drawing a broad range of input and virtually universal support. The term 'human rights' might not be explicitly used in many cultures but the concepts that became codified as human rights certainly are. A smaller drafting panel was formed, chaired by Charles Malik, who was Lebanese.

The context was the immediate post Second World War (1939-1945) period. The three major victorious powers, the Soviet Union, the United States and the United Kingdom, each had major internal issues with the concept of human rights. The Soviet Union was operating Gulags and enforcing collectivisation. For the United States, the 1940s predate the rise of the Civil Rights Movement and the different treatment of people based on their colour was rife in parts of the country. For the United Kingdom, there was the British Empire, many of whose peoples had been exploited as cheap labour. Was the UK really willing to now assert that such peoples had the same rights, privileges and duties as themselves?

In contrast, there was a strong international consensus to respond to the irrefutable evidence of the Holocaust and other major abuses of human beings seen during the Second World War. The view that the actions of one state should be subject to examination by others rapidly became accepted, motivated by the desire to prevent genocide and other serious crimes against humanity from being perpetrated in the future.

Charles Malik pushed the process to a conclusion in December 1948. He sensed that rising tensions in Berlin, the Korean Peninsula and the Middle East were likely to make securing widespread international agreement on anything increasingly more difficult. In his judgement, the window of opportunity for such agreements following the Second World War was about to close and he needed to act decisively, quickly and inclusively.

The declaration is a carefully crafted balance of the rights of individuals and the rights of communities. Charles Malik, in his address to the United Nations General Assembly on 10th December 1948, publicly thanked the Soviet member of the panel for articulating the communal aspects so clearly. This speech preceded the assembly's vote to formally adopt the United Nations Universal Declaration of Human Rights.

When the UN General Assembly voted on the declaration, there were 47 votes in favour, no votes against and eight abstentions. The eight abstainers were Belorussia, Czechoslovakia, Poland, the Republic of South Africa, Saudi Arabia, the Soviet Union, Ukraine and Yugoslavia. Of note is that Saudi Arabia is the only predominantly-Muslim state in this list.

These observations counter the assertion made by some that the declaration, and indeed the whole concept of human rights, is a Western agenda imposed on the rest of the world. The drafting process was widely based, with a broad consensus for the concept. A Lebanese man played a leading role and there is a communal element complementing the rights of individuals. As we noted earlier, the balance of individual and communal rights is crucial for religious expression.

Three aspects of human rights are crucial. First, that they are *universal*, in that they apply to all human beings. Second, they are *inalienable*, that is, they apply irrespective of circumstances. Third, they are *indivisible*, *interrelated* and *interdependent*; if one right is denied there are significant effects on other rights. In the next chapter, we will see that religious registration is an example of this.

Today we see challenges to the universality of human rights emanating from four principal sources. The first challenge comes from repressive regimes. In the founding of the United Nations it was recognised that humanity had a duty to monitor the actions of rulers to ensure that large scale violations of rights were exposed and responded to. This continues to be the case, although we must note that some repressive regimes resist such attention and there are numerous constraints on effective international intervention. In recent years the concept of Responsibility to Protect (R2P for short) has emerged. Again, the constraints on international intervention are immense.[38]

The second challenge arises out of what I will term egotism, namely a combination of sources encouraging individuals to do whatever they wish. This egotistical threat originated in a combination of post-modern Western culture and extremist secularism. At root, it denies the true humanity of some individuals.

The third challenge is from religious radicalism, which typically attempts to assert that some have greater

[38] See for example Gareth Evans's book *Responsibility to Protect* published by Brookings Institute in 2008.

rights than others. This is particularly prevalent in the Islamic world, notably where extremist groups exert influence. We noted in chapter 10 that the Arab Awakening is stimulating debate in many countries about the nature of the state. One expression of this is in the constitutions, to which we will return in chapter 26.

The fourth challenge is from rising nationalism and fears of excessive migration. Immigration has become a potent topic in political debate in many Western countries. Shami Chakravarti's book *On Liberty* asks the probing question of whether we wish to be protected as human beings everywhere or to be treated as citizens in our own countries and foreigners abroad, i.e. having greater rights and protections in different places. Her book can be viewed as a defence of the universal nature of human rights.[39]

So, if the Universal Declaration of Human Rights of 1948 is the foundation of the modern era of human rights, then what happened next? What was built on

---

[39] Published by Penguin Books in 2014

the foundation that it laid? What continues to be built on it? This story continues in the following chapter.

Chapter 25

International Covenants

The Universal Declaration of Human Rights is, as it says, a declaration. Strictly speaking, it summarises the views of those who endorsed it in December 1948. Whilst it carries moral weight, it has no legal authority or force, although some argue that it has such moral weight that it can be regarded as having legal authority within international law. What do have legal force, in some senses, are the two international covenants that are directly derived from it, namely the International Covenant on Civil and Political Rights (ICCPR) and the International Covenant on Economic, Social and Cultural Rights. Simplistically, the former covers the rights of individuals and the latter the rights of communities. These two documents were formally adopted in 1966.

These two covenants articulate in more detail what the rights, responsibilities and duties of citizens and legitimate authorities are. As with the Declaration, the drafting process was very broadly based, and took a considerable period of time.

Each covenant invites every UN member state to become a 'State Party.' This is typically effected by a representative of the state signing the covenant on behalf of the nation. The country's legislative process then enacts into national law the state's commitment to uphold the provisions of the covenant. This process is summarised as 'signing' and 'ratifying' the covenant. A shorter but equally binding process is 'acceding' to a covenant which typically involves the head of state using his/her executive authority to commit the state to uphold the covenant.

A covenant itself becomes operative when a stated number of countries complete this process. At this point, a United Nations committee is established that oversees the implementation and interpretation of the covenant by State Parties, i.e. those countries that have formally ratified or acceded to the covenant.

What is stated about religious belief?

Article 18 of the Universal Declaration of Human Rights states that:

> Everyone has the right to freedom of thought, conscience and religion; this right includes freedom to change his religion or belief, and freedom, either alone or in community with others and in public or

private, to manifest his religion or belief in teaching, practice, worship and observance.

This article was treated as being more about individuals than communities and so placed in the ICCPR, where it is again Article 18. We will discuss the balance between individuals and communities in the expression of religious belief in chapter 28.

Article 18 of the International Covenant on Civil and Political Rights reads as follows:

1. Everyone shall have the right to freedom of thought, conscience and religion. This right shall include freedom to have or to adopt a religion or belief of his choice, and freedom, either individually or in community with others and in public or private, to manifest his religion or belief in worship, observance, practice and teaching.

2. No one shall be subject to coercion which would impair his freedom to have or to adopt a religion or belief of his choice.

3. Freedom to manifest one's religion or beliefs may be subject only to such limitations as are prescribed by law and are

necessary to protect public safety, order, health, or morals or the fundamental rights and freedoms of others.

4. The States Parties to the present Covenant undertake to have respect for the liberty of parents and, when applicable, legal guardians to ensure the religious and moral education of their children in conformity with their own convictions.

Much is made by some that the word 'change' is not used in this article of the covenant when it was used in the Universal Declaration of Human Rights. Why? Is this significant?

For why, it reflects the use of slightly weaker language in order to achieve widespread agreement. As we have noted during our tour of the region, religious conversion can be controversial. Covenants, including this one, endeavour to be short, succinct yet broad in addressing their subject area. Consequently, they seek brevity in use of language.

Is it significant? Not really, because the underlying intention is clear that the covenant includes the right to change from one faith to another. This can be seen in the minutes of the drafting committee's meetings and by looking at how the wording has consistently been interpreted since it was finalised in 1966. Further, the official comments and statements issued by the UN committee that oversees the implementation of this covenant consistently uphold the view that the word 'adopt' in the covenant includes the right to convert from one faith to another. This is also true of the comments and reports issued by the UN Special Rappateur for Religious Intolerance. (The UN has established a number of Special Rappateur posts covering either a special topic within human rights, religious freedom in this case, or focussed on a specific country, e.g. The Special Rappateur on Iran, a post currently held by Ahmad Shaheed.)

Religious freedom can be viewed as operating at several levels. First, the essence of being human requires the ability to investigate the origin and meaning of human existence, and to adopt a belief of one's choosing. Thus religious freedom is a foundational human right, operating alongside freedom of conscience, expression and opinion. These underpin the concept of freedom of the press, which is crucial for holding political, community, business and religious leaders to account. As we saw in chapter 10, this is a crucial issue in many parts of the Middle East at this time since one theme of the Arab Awakening is a call for an end to corruption, nepotism and cronyism.

Second, the fundamental freedom to have or to adopt a religion or belief of one's choice may not be subject to any limitations. The provisions of the ICCPR allow the freedom to manifest one's religion or belief to be subject to limitations. In other words, the communal aspects of religious freedom may be limited but not the individual aspects.

Third, religious freedom requires that all citizens be able to manifest their faith alone or with others, in private or public. This includes the right of individuals to enter and leave religious communities, and to put their faith into the public space with an invitation that others may choose to join the group. This right must be exercised in a manner that respects the rights of others, which implies that there can be no coercion, inducements or other undue pressure. We referred to this in chapter 13 when we discussed forced conversion and ethical proselytising.

It is implied that all religious groups should be able to become and operate as legally recognised entities, and that there should be equality amongst religious groups in regulations concerning places of worship.

Fourth, all citizens have the right to take their religious faith into the public sphere to inform public policy debate. It is a common feature of many faiths that the ethical aspects of the faith should impact all aspects of life. This is true of Judaism, Christianity and Islam.

In recent years the phrase 'Freedom of Religion or Belief' has become more widely used, at least within human rights circles. This phrase overtly recognises that proponents of belief systems such as humanism, atheism, communism and secularism need and utilise the same freedoms that religious adherents utilise. They too need to meet with fellow adherents, write about their beliefs and communicate about their beliefs in public places. It is sometimes argued that humanists and secularists are less aware of their use of such rights than are adherents of religions. True pluralism welcomes the contributions of adherents of all religions and beliefs.

As is often said, theory is one thing but what happens in practice? What enforcement mechanisms apply to international law and how effective are they? This is the subject of the next chapter.

Chapter 26

Constitutions, National and International Law

During our regional tour we have noticed a few places in which international and national law have clashed. For example, in Turkey we noted that two rulings by the European Court of Human Rights had not been implemented, one concerning the Alevi and the other the removal of religious registration from identity cards.

We also noted in Israel that national law was being overridden by religious law; one example being the religious authorities refusing to issue a kosher certificate to a bakery despite an order by the Supreme Court to do so.

We will return to these questions and also examine the role of constitutions with respect to religious freedom and the clear rule of law applied equally to all, one theme of the Arab Awakening.

It is often asked how international law is enforced. Certainly, enforcement is different from that of national law. I do wonder if 'enforcement' is the most appropriate term.

International norms (a subtle change of terminology) can be viewed as stating what humanity as a whole regards as best practice. This alerts and informs people what they should expect, gives them an agreed language for such expectations and enables them to seek to improve their situation. With today's communication tools the phrase 'be a voice for the voiceless'[40] could be supplemented by 'enable those who think that they are voiceless to be able to express themselves.' This involves listening, recording, translating (if required) and facilitating the use of online mechanisms of expression. It remains true that some are unable to speak for themselves. One example is those imprisoned for their beliefs, although some are able to pass messages via visitors enabling their voice to be heard on global online media.

Returning to enforcement, the consequences of a state violating international norms are often in the areas of public opinion and inter-state relations. Some countries, notably those who are members of the European Union, include respect for human rights

---

[40] A number of Christian organisations base their use of the phrase 'voice for the voiceless' on Proverbs 31:8 and Isaiah 1:17

standards and norms in international trade agreements. The concept of fair trade is relevant in this context as an international mechanism that protects the vulnerable from being exploited by the powerful. The use of labelling systems to facilitate informed choices by people worldwide of whether to buy products and services from specific locations is another method by which the international community demonstrates its acceptance or rejection of the practices of others.

In April 2008 the United Nations Human Rights Council conducted the first meetings of its Universal Periodic Review system. In this system, every UN member is the subject of a peer review of its human rights record. The review process begins with written submissions being made by the government under scrutiny. Other states and Non-Government Organisations (NGOs, or charities) may also make written submissions. A meeting is conducted by the Council at which the written submissions are examined and differences of opinion are discussed and evaluated. The council considers all points of view and writes a report summarising the discussions and recommendations for improvements in the areas of concern. The government under review is expected to make a written response, either accepting or rejecting each recommendation.

This system exposes all countries (except the very few who are not members of the UN) to review in the court of international attention every four years. It is now typical for each review to include discussion of actions taken to address the recommendations made during the previous review.

Another change that has occurred in recent years is the establishment of the International Criminal Court. This was created by the Rome Statute of 17th July 1998 with a mandate to prosecute individuals on charges relating to gross violations of human rights. The Court formally came into being on 1st July 2002 based in The Hague, Netherlands when the sixtieth nation ratified the Rome Statute and became a State Party to the Court. The Court's mandate covers genocide, war crimes, crimes against humanity and crimes of aggression, although the latter will only become operative in 2017 at the earliest.

The Court's first injunction issued against a serving head of state occurred on 13th July 2010 when judges at the Court issued a warrant for President Omar Hassan al-Bashir of Sudan on charges of genocide relating to his government's actions in Darfur, western Sudan. President Bashir remains at liberty, although he has, on occasions, adjusted his travel schedule due to the realisation that he might be arrested and transferred to The Hague whenever he visits a country that is a State Party to the Court.

The Court has issued charges against others involved in Darfur, including some who used violent methods in opposition to the government. In the case of Darfur, the Court has overtly fulfilled its mandate to uphold justice for all parties to a conflict. In 2010 two such men, Saleh Mohammed Jerbo Jamus and Abdallah Banda Abakaer Nourain, surrendered to the Court and voluntarily flew to The Hague. They were charged with war crimes relating to the killing of 12 African Union (AU) peacekeepers in an attack on the AU's Haskanita camp in September 2007. In view of their cooperation, they were released on bail. In March 2011 the judges at a pre-trial hearing concluded that there was sufficient evidence to warrant a trial which was scheduled to commence during 2014. However, in April 2013 Jamus' lawyers announced that he had been killed during fighting in northern Darfur. In September 2014 the Court asked the Sudanese government to arrest and surrender Nourain. At the time of writing, he remains at large.

To summarise, the enforcement of international law is different from that of national law. The mechanisms available to the international community are less direct and rarely (if ever) have immediate effect, but, over time they produce observable results. Many governments have amended their legal systems in response to public scrutiny under the UN or as part of agreeing to international trade agreements. The International Criminal Court has led to changed behaviour by Sudan's president, although not as yet to the extent desired by many Sudanese citizens, notably those forcibly displaced from the Darfur region.

Recall that Magna Carta was signed in 1215 and it took a considerable period of time before its provisions became the daily reality of all citizens. I trust that the modern system of human rights will not take so long!

Those involved in supporting Christian communities when their rights are violated for religious reasons frequently use the language of human rights. This is also true for nationals who respond to such violations by standing up for their rights. International norms give them an awareness that they do have rights and a language to use in asking that these rights be respected.

When a person's rights are violated for religious or other reasons, or a combination of reasons, they can respond in one of three ways. In the Introduction we entitled these 'accept,' 'resist' or 'leave.' In most cases each option has its attractions and also potential costs and risks. One can simply acknowledge the injustice and choose to accept it and live with whatever consequences it brings. Typically, these will include suffering the same injustice again, or watching others suffer in a similar manner. The couple in the Arabian Peninsula (chapter 22) chose this alternative, having enquired about resisting the injustice they faced by submitting a court case. Resisting injustice means standing up for one's self and those in similar situations. Siham (chapter 1) and Mohammed Hegazy (chapter 2) are examples whose cases lasted several years. One was resolved (at least to a large extent), the other was not. The final possible course of action is to leave the situation. This option has long-term consequences and is usually more difficult than it appears. So, it should be regarded as the option of last resort, only to be used if acceptance and resistance are not viable. Ramzi and Muna (chapter 1) are a couple who were obliged to leave their country, changing the certainty of turmoil for a turmoil of uncertainty.

In standing up for one's rights, many refer to their nation's constitution. One example we noted was Mohammed Hegazy's challenge to Egypt's religious registration system (chapter 2). Constitutions serve different purposes in different cultural contexts. In Western democracies, a country's constitution is the highest form of law, shaping the governance structure, penal code and family law. The relative powers of the different branches of national government are clearly defined, as is the balance of powers between national and lower levels of governance at local, municipal and regional/provincial levels. Such constitutions can be changed, but the process to do so is usually complex. There is a legal mechanism that ensures that all legislation is compatible, often named as the Supreme Court or the Constitutional Court.

In other contexts, the constitution serves as a guide or as an expression of intent. Some seek to preserve the privileges of elite groups or the architects of the document. An example of this is Iraq's 2005 constitution whose main architects were the Shi'a and the Kurds who both ensured that their primary interests were covered. For the Shi'a these were provision for Shari'a law and to ensure access to a fair amount of the water resources since they are downstream of the Kurdish and Sunni areas. The Kurds' interests were different, namely to formalise the status of their autonomous region administered by the Kurdish Regional Government, to provide a mechanism for Kirkuk to become included in this region, and provision for a Western style legal system as they had no desire for Shari'a based law. The constitution therefore includes provision for both Shari'a and non-Shari'a based law. It seeks to ensure a fair distribution of natural resources, notably water and oil, without specifying how this is to be achieved.

One major concern of many Sunnis is the reference to de-Baath-ification which continues to exclude many Sunnis from government employment. A revision of the de-Baath-ification law was passed in January 2008, barring former Baathist party members of the top three (as opposed to the previous four) of the party's six levels from government positions, theoretically allowing as many as 30,000 people to apply for government jobs. During the Saddam

Hussein era many Sunnis held Baath Party membership primarily motivated by their need for employment rather than because of any ideological support for the governing party or its leader.

Elsewhere in the Middle East, several countries have amended their constitutions since the start of the Arab Awakening. Egypt has made three revisions in as many years. The third revision was prepared during autumn 2013 and approved in a national referendum on 16th January 2014. Under this constitution the state guarantees "equality between men and women," which addresses a major concern with the previous constitution. The December 2012 constitution lacked clarity at several points and internal inconsistency would have allowed a hard line interpretation of Shari'a to be imposed as certain clauses could over-ride provisions made elsewhere. In the January 2014 constitution freedom of belief is made an absolute right of all citizens, although Islam remains the state religion. Consequently, the issue that underlies the Mohammed Hegazy case that we discussed in chapter 2 remains. Does the stipulation of Shari'a as the principal source of legislation mean that religious registration cannot be changed to reflect a person's choice of religious belief? Alternatively, does freedom of belief being an absolute right imply that religious registration should be changeable in all directions? At some point the legal consideration underlying the Hegazy case will be resumed.

One serious concern is that the constitution allows military trials of civilians, which is contrary to international norms. This reflects the military's key role in preparing this version of the constitution. As with Iraq in 2005, the key stakeholders are preserving their privileges. As we noted in chapter 10 on the Arab Awakening, it will be some years yet before a fuller expression of international norms on human rights is enshrined in Egypt's constitution and, more significantly, in the daily experience of all Egyptians.

We conclude this chapter with a brief reflection on what is meant by a national religion. Egypt's constitution, like most Middle Eastern countries, asserts that Islam is the state religion. In many countries, one form of Islam is given preferential treatment over all others. For example in Saudi Arabia the Wahhabi tradition of Sunni Islam is favoured whilst Shi'a Islam is regarded as second class and its adherents are disadvantaged in government employment.

Throughout history, where there is a state religion, typically the political powers have manipulated, pressured and controlled the religious authorities to bless and endorse whatever the political power decides to do. There are privileges in being the state religion; there are also costs.

On 4th December 2013 the National Assembly of Libya voted to make Shari'a the source of all legislation. This was presented as a manoeuvre by moderate Islamists and ultra-conservative militants to influence the future of Libya. It came at a time when a more conservative viewpoint was gaining influence, partly due to the actions of armed groups. Those from the moderate position noted that the legal system contains very few laws that contradict Shari'a. During the Colonel Qaddafi era there had been a review of the legal code with a view of ensuring that it was Shari'a compliant. Consequently, they foresaw little need for radical changes. They viewed the Assembly vote as a symbolic act which would have little actual effect. Subsequent events during 2014 overshadowed such considerations.

This prompts the question as to whether it is religious clerics or political decision makers who determine what is Shari'a compliant and what is not. Is the religious view decisive or are the religious leaders being pressured to endorse the political leaders' decisions? The balance of powers is not always obvious.

At this point we can return to one of our opening questions. Why, in Israel, can a 'Supreme Court' ruling be ignored with impunity by a religious authority? Israel is a state where the position of the state religion is unclear. Strictly speaking, the state is secular, i.e. political decision making is independent of all religious authorities, but religious authorities have been given authority in personal status matters. What we observed in the case of the bakery can be viewed in several ways.

One is that a religious authority is exerting authority in a civil matter, i.e. a dispute between citizens. This is questionable, since it is not clear where the boundary is between religious and civil matters; the religious authority is asserting control of compliance with religiously-derived food standards, whereas the state and the baker are claiming that this should be governed by the national food standards.

Another view is that this relates to acknowledgement (or not!) of the difference between ethnicity – Jewish

– and religion – Judaism. Ethnicity is an inherent characteristic and unchangeable; in contrast, religious adherence can be changed and some people do convert. The religious authority is stating that a convert cannot be trusted, whereas the state and the applicant are stating that compliance with food standards should be based on observed behaviour.

We conclude this discussion by noting that the state has declined to charge the religious authority with contempt of court, nor has it amended the law to clarify the jurisdiction of religious courts. The baker is left without justice; religious law has trumped national law; the state is complicit in permitting this outcome. As we asked earlier, in what senses is Israel a secular state, a Jewish state or a state governed by Judaism?

A converse example can be seen in Turkey. We noted in chapter 5 that the government favours one branch of Sunni Islam over other forms of Islam and other religions despite the state's founding document clearly separating state and religion.

Our other opening question was why Turkey can apparently ignore with impunity some rulings handed down by the European Court of Human Rights. This

Court is an instrument of the Council of Europe, which Turkey joined within three months of its founding on 5th May 1949. The Court's rulings are, in theory, binding on all members of the Council.

Turkey is applying for EU membership, a process that it initiated in 1959. There are numerous factors at work in the long-running saga of Turkey's application. One consequence of it becoming a member would be that Turkey would be obliged to treat the Court's rulings with the utmost respect because one aspect of EU membership is to formalise into national law that the Court's rulings must be taken seriously.

At present there are no effective enforcement mechanisms applicable to Turkey, and so refusal to respect the rulings has had minimal direct consequences in some cases. In chapter 5 we did note that in one case a ruling by the Court about Cemevis facilitated a course of action being taken locally to seek the desired recognition of these places of worship for Alevi communities. This is an example of international norms facilitating local action to confront injustice.

The role of constitutions is not always what it appears and the balance of power amongst various political and religious bodies is not easy to discern. Both factors mitigate against the clear rule of law applied equally to all, one aspiration of the Arab Awakening, creating uncertainty for society. These factors further complicate addressing the pluralism deficit.

My own country, the UK, has a state religion, or more precisely, a state-branch-of-one-religion, namely the Anglican church. Historically, this religious body played a role in the development of religious pluralism in the UK, first allowing the Roman Catholic church due recognition. Recognition of other Protestant denominations followed; the collective term "non-conformist" is sometimes used for them since they do not conform to the patterns of religious practice embraced by the 'state religion.' Later came allowance for Judaism to establish synagogues, followed by adherents of other world faiths. At some point allowance was made for atheists. Of relevance to the Middle East is the example of a state religion playing a significant role in the development of pluralism.

Having looked at the theoretical and practical outworking of international norms, we can review our tour of the Middle East and summarise our observations of how the religious registration system and its effects measure up against these norms.

Chapter 27

Religious Registration Against Norms

So how do we assess the challenges and flash points of religious registration against international norms? We consider some general applications before looking at several country specific challenges noted during our regional tour.

One immediate challenge concerns the international norm that an individual's change of religion should be respected. Many people desire to mark major transitions in life such as marriage, the birth of children and burial using religious rites of passage. Religious registration determines which rite is applicable, yet the options for those who choose to follow a different faith are restricted, notably those who become Christians from other faiths. Consequently, religious registration should be changeable in all directions. In January 2014 Iraqi church leaders became the first Christian leaders in the Middle East to call for this to become the norm (chapter 18).

A corollary of this is that apostasy should not be a crime. This is not to overlook the social implications of an individual's change of religion, or of a nuclear family making such a decision. We need to keep in mind that a change of religion will affect which communities within society people closely identify with and how they affirm, support and nourish their sense of identity and belonging. There are always consequences for those who convert: these are social and communal, but not criminal. Apostasy should not be a crime.

It is also the case that nobody should be arrested, charged, convicted and sentenced for legitimate Christian activities. In our tour we noted that this is all too common in Iran and also occurs in Algeria. Apostasy charges might have been dropped; other charges have been used instead. This is equally inconsistent with international norms. In June 2011 the UN appointed Dr. Ahmed Shaheed as their "Special Rapporteur on the Situation of Human Rights in the Islamic Republic of Iran." Dr. Shaheed's report of 13th September 2012 included a summary of violations of religious freedom experienced by Iran's Baha'i, Christian and Sufi communities.[41]

---

[41] Dr. Ahmed Shaheed's website is
http://www.shaheedoniran.org/english/ (accessed 5th May 2015)

Another area in which religious registration and international norms clash is that of marriage. The current practice prevalent in many countries restricts women whose religious registration is Muslim from marrying a non-Muslim. To meet international norms either the restriction should be lifted or people should be allowed to change their religious registration. It is insufficient to assert that men are obliged to become Muslim in order to marry a woman whose registration is Muslim – there should be no coercion in religion. The calls during the Arab Awakening suggest that younger generations across the region desire the freedom to marry whom they choose. Some would welcome the introduction of civil marriage as a complement to religiously-based procedures. When will legislators make this a reality?

A related area is the international norm of parental choice in the religious education of children. There is no such choice in most Middle Eastern countries for those whose registration is Muslim but yet have become adherents of Christianity.

Religious meetings in homes, which is common in much Christian practice, is affirmed by international norms. In many Middle Eastern countries religious meetings in homes are illegal – in chapter 5 we noted

Turkey as an example of this. Such laws are frequently designed to control Muslim cells some of which the authorities fear might consider adopting violent methods. In some countries, such laws are implemented with considerable discretion. In Morocco, the law forbids meetings of more than ten people in a home. This is usually taken to mean ten guests plus the resident family, but extended family gatherings frequently exceed this limit. Determining what is a family gathering and what is a religious meeting is not always obvious.

The international norm is that religions can teach the faith to adherents, with the implication that future leaders can be trained. This is problematic in some countries due to the denial of seminaries (e.g. in Turkey) or restrictions on less formal methods of instruction. Christians, as well as members of other faiths, regard passing on the faith to the next generation as crucial. A related issue is the ability to create, produce and distribute suitable training materials, including materials for children of all ages. If governments formally identify people as Christians then it seems somewhat inconsistent to place restrictions on how such people teach their children either individually at home or collectively within Christian communities.

Having considered some general applications, we now move to a few country specific issues. We will start in Jordan, as did our tour of the region, before proceeding to Egypt and elsewhere.

In Jordan we noted that Shari'a courts have annulled every document ever signed by Ramzi and several others, thereby removing all their civil rights and protections before the whole of Jordanian law. It is stating the obvious that this falls far short of acceptability under international norms. Judaism, Christianity and Islam are all holistic religions, i.e. religious beliefs inform all aspects of the lives of their adherents, both as individuals and collectively as part of religious communities that are part of wider society. Nevertheless, a religious court's jurisdiction should not extend beyond specifically religious matters. So, Shari'a courts, and any other religious court, should only be applicable in situations where everyone involved willingly accepts their jurisdiction and agrees to abide by their rulings.

In Siham's case, the custody issue was resolved but she was deprived of her widow's benefit. Effectively, the government has denied Siham the state benefits owing to her as the widow of someone who died whilst serving with the military. The government also initiated the forced change of religious registration for a family, in apparent contradiction to the law used by Siham's children. What effect does such capricious inconsistency have on Jordanian society in general and its Christian community in particular?

It remains my opinion that Jordan is the worst country in the Middle East for how its legal system treats those whose religious registration is Muslim but who choose to become Christians.

In Egypt, there are separate laws regulating the requirements to build or repair mosques and church buildings, leading to extreme discrepancies between how Muslims and Christians are treated. Article 235 of the constitutional revision approved in January 2014 instructs parliament to enact legislation giving equal treatment under planning laws for places of worship for the 'heavenly religions,' i.e. Islam, Christianity and Judaism. Such legislation was discussed during 2011 by senior Christian leaders and the Grand Mufti. An initial draft of such a bill was prepared more than 18 years ago.

We noted in chapter 17 that church architecture and buildings carry cultural and theological importance for many Christians in the Middle East and are integral to rites and worship for many churches. This is true for the Coptic Orthodox Church in Egypt. Church buildings also confer recognition of a place within society and hence contribute to a sense of identity for Christians. This is true for many Protestant churches in Egypt as well as the Orthodox and Catholic churches. Can we say that the places of worship legislation would be a significant contribution towards the realisation of the hope expressed in Tahrir Square for all Egyptians to be equal citizens? Would it not contribute to addressing the pluralism deficit?

One subtle observation is that, at the time of writing, the Egyptian government also discriminates against some of its Muslim communities. Will mosques for Shi'a be given equal treatment to those for Sunni? To do so would make Egypt a model for addressing the intra-Islam pluralism deficit prevalent in much of the Arab world.

In chapter 2 we noted that the legal challenge to the religious registration system initiated by Mohammed Hegazy was allowed to lapse by the Constitutional

Court. We can ask who has the authority to reinstate the proceedings? Clearly the court could do so itself. One wonders whether they prefer to let it lie dormant rather than rule in favour of Christians for fear of a backlash within Egypt or rule against Christians out of concern for a critical reaction from the West. The President or the government could intervene. They can with some degree of legitimacy state that they are respecting judicial independence, although such interference in the justice system has been only too common in the past.

Finally, we should consider the role of the Grand Mufti, i.e. the recognised spiritual leader of Sunni Islam in Egypt. The Grand Mufti also holds the position of head of Al-Azhar University, the leading academic authority within Sunni Islam. In some senses, he is an international religious figure as well as a national religious leader. The judicial system would most likely place a high weight to any opinion the Grand Mufti were to express, whether done discreetly or publicly. The balance of power between state and religion is not always clear.

Algerian Christians continue to discuss the 2006 law on non-Muslim worship with their government. They seek administrative procedures that enable churches to register and procedures that uphold the country's commitment to there being no discrimination based on religion. They seek withdrawal of the provisions on evangelism on the grounds that it is legitimate for anyone to express their religious belief to those who inquire, and to place knowledge of the faith in the public arena with an open invitation for others to choose to become fellow adherents.

One final general point is worth noting, although it primarily relates to the understanding, or rather the misunderstanding, of religious freedom outside the Middle East. We have noticed several examples of people leaving the region in response to religiously-motivated persecution. Ramzi and Muna are one example. It is sometimes said to Christians whose religious registration is Muslim within refugee and asylum systems that they could live in their own country if they just kept quiet about their faith. This is a clear restriction on their religious freedom. They are being told to exercise their faith in private and alone, whereas the international norm includes with others and in a place of public worship.

We have noted the difference between international norms and the current practice of religious registration in the Middle East. Now we can consider in what ways this system is a blessing on society and in what ways it is a curse. This is unlikely to prove straightforward but is crucial to our task of 'finding a way through.'

Chapter 28

Is Religious Registration a Blessing or Curse in the Middle East?

So how does religious registration affect societies across the Middle East? Do people in the Middle East typically see it as a blessing, as a curse, or just as the way things are? Does it help or hinder multi-religious and multi-ethnic peoples to live together well?

Does it help or hinder Christians, and adherents of other faiths, in living well where they are? Does it build and affirm their sense of identity and belonging in the Middle East? What part does it play in either enabling them to remain or does it push them to leave?

There are no simple yes/no answers to these questions.

Our regional tour has focussed more on the negative consequences for some Christians. In contrast, this chapter dwells more on the benefits. It also focuses on the communal aspects of religious registration rather than its effect on individuals.

For Christian communities, we might summarise the situation as being a blessing for those whose primary focus is the pastoral role of the church. For such people, it identifies those for whom there is official approval for them to provide friendship and support. To use a religious metaphor, it identifies the sheep and the sheepfold for those the church has designated as shepherds.

It also identifies those whom such people need to be cautious about supporting, namely those whose registration is other than Christian who approach a church leader looking for support. They can respond to such people as human beings. They, and those who make requests of them, are aware that in many parts of the Middle East there are risks for both parties in such approaches.

On 18th November 2012 Bishop Tawadros was inaugurated as Pope Tawadros II, Head of the Coptic Orthodox Church in Egypt. One of Pope Tawadros II's first actions was to encourage Egyptian Christians to become actively engaged in all levels of politics. No longer would the church act as their representative. Instead, Christians should involve themselves in political processes to address the concerns of their communities within Egyptian society as a whole. Pope

Tawadros also encouraged members of the Coptic Orthodox Church to interact with Christians from other traditions. This created a tension within the Orthodox Church between traditional and conservative members and those willing to be more open to Christians of other traditions. This is being open to those whose religious registration is not identical to their own; religious registration has intra-religion aspects!

The announcement of President Morsi's removal from office on 3rd July 2013 was made by the head of the Supreme Military Council flanked by Pope Tawrados II and the Grand Mufti. The two religious leaders represented the people as the military authority asserted control of the country in response (as we saw in chapter 10) to a groundswell of public opinion. The Pope accepted this public platform for a key political event. He has steadfastly followed the course he established in November 2012 of encouraging Egyptian Christians to participate in political processes, acting as citizens, seeking to establish good governance at all levels for the benefit of all Egyptians. He is asking that Christians be citizens first and holders of a religious registration of Christian second, whilst remaining faithful in religious belief and practice. Further, religious belief and practice inform attitudes and behaviour in daily life, and contribute to public debate on the issues of the day. He is giving a model to follow and one for which religious registration is not required.

We noted in chapters 17 and 27 that the Egyptian church strongly desires amendment of the planning regulations to give parity for churches and mosques. The church as an institution has not yet succeeded in achieving this. So, perhaps the time is right to try another approach. I acknowledge that the context in which the Egyptian church has been obliged to operate in recent decades was complex and challenging – appendix 4 gives some of the reasons for this. The Arab Awakening is a changing context; the future does not have to look like the past. Is this a suitable time to ask for justice, generosity and equality to prevail in this area?

In at least two countries – Turkey and Sudan – religious registration has been cited by the authorities as a factor in considering the status of church property and of applications for some new church buildings. In Turkey, the authorities check the membership of some groups applying for a building, using religious registration to check that they have a viable group of people identifying themselves as Christian in order to be able to operate a place of worship. Turkish citizens are able to change their religious registration although social and cultural pressures mitigate against individuals exercising such a right. In Sudan, the authorities have stated that there are fewer Christians because many have moved to South Sudan (or elsewhere) and consequently fewer places of Christian worship are required. Factors such as actual attendance figures or Christians moving to new housing developments in major towns and cities are disregarded. Can we argue that this use of religious registration by Turkey has some degree of legitimacy whereas the Sudanese usage does not?

We also need to ask what is the effect on the church's role of being a prophetic voice, of being able to speak truth to power. In recent decades, Church leaders have been left in no doubt that certain subjects were taboo, a situation that applied equally strongly to others – in many Middle Eastern countries political dissent and critical comment on the actions of rulers led to serious consequences; there were too many 'political prisoners.' One theme of the Arab Awakening is to call for an end to this situation. Public opinion is being heard and taken due note of. In such a context, Christian communities throughout the Middle East have an opportunity to find appropriate means of expression that enables a critique of the powerful to be made. Whether this is in public discourse or in private meetings of church leaders with senior government officials might vary from country to country and from topic to topic.

Another Old Testament theme is worthy of note at this point. These Hebrew scriptures present God as loving of all ethnic groups. The Israelites are chosen to be an example, to show what God is like and how he expects everyone to live. The emphasis is that being chosen is primarily about responsibilities, not privileges. They have an allocated place to be, and their continued presence in that space is dependent on the ethical standards by which they live. In his book *Healing Wounded History* Russ Parker argues that these principles apply across humanity, i.e. to groups within society as well as to national governance.[42] This is an injunction for Christians to be involved in ensuring that all communities of which they are part live wisely in accordance with the

---

[42] Published by D.L.T. in 2001

character of God himself. Hospitality, generosity and a welcome for strangers are part of this mandate.

In the light of this consideration, how do we view religious registration? Does it help or hinder Christian communities in the fulfilment of this aspect of its mandate? Our answer to this might be mixed: it does identify who is a stranger, and in many Middle Eastern contexts, providing hospitality for strangers has become counter-cultural – the norm being to look after one's own. Consequently, being generous to strangers is counter-cultural and hence memorable to the recipients.

We note that one step could be to remove religious registration from identity documents, as the Palestinian Authority did in February 2014 (chapter 16). While such a change might reduce some forms of societal discrimination, restrictions will still apply until confessionally-based personal status law is complemented by a civil system. An alternative approach would be for change of religious registration to become unrestricted, allowing all citizens to choose the faith and legal system whose jurisdiction they wish to abide by. This would leave the challenges faced by atheists unresolved, forcing them to use religiously-based rites.

Yet we must acknowledge that many leaders of officially recognised Christian communities (as well as other religious communities) would oppose the removal of the religious designation or a move away from confessionally based personal status laws. They consider this to be an important aspect of maintaining their Christian identity and affording Christians protection within Church structures. Any consideration of dropping the religious identity would need to take account of the wider concerns of Christian communities and be introduced alongside measures to address the pluralism deficit, notably measures to affirm that Christian communities are a valued and integral part of society.

What is the way through?

We noted in chapter 8 that Christians in Jordan were regarded by senior figures as crucial to the fabric of society, as the glue that held the country together. So, we move from discussing how religious registration affects Christian communities to asking how it affects the society of which they are a part.

One pertinent question is whether religious affiliation is an individual or communal matter. This is more complex than it might appear. Religion as a belief system is clearly an individual matter; yet religious practice in teaching and worship has a corporate dimension. There is a fundamental element of identification with a group of likeminded people.

In many communities, the religious affiliation of each individual is regarded as part of the collective identity of the group, of the community, whether that is the nuclear family, the extended family, the clan or the whole ethnic group. Consequently, an individual becoming an adherent of another faith is a major event in the life of the group. It is perceived as leaving the group, as a betrayal. At root, this is one reason why apostasy is taken seriously.

Those from non-Christian backgrounds who choose to become Christians are frequently advised not to tell immediate family members of their choice too soon. They are advised to adapt their attitudes and behaviour to reflect the ethical outworking of their new faith. If asked, they are encouraged not to lie or be deceitful, either of which are likely to provoke a strong adverse reaction (as we noted in chapter 13). When the realisation comes and the choice becomes known, then family members will have seen the difference that becoming a Christian has made to how they conduct themselves as well as experiencing the feelings of rejection and betrayal that are an inevitable consequence of the communal nature of the society. In time, for most such Christians, their immediate family members come to accept and respect their choice and resume an appropriate family relationship, though there are exceptions.

The picture is less clear for wider family. We noted that for Ramzi, it was his brothers in-law who assaulted him, which in turn created the pressure on his father to seek custody of the children. This is a typical pattern of events, i.e. it is wider family, not immediate family, members who initiate strong actions against converts.

It is clear that an individual's religious affiliation has an effect on the communities of which they are a part.

Along our journey we encountered the concept of apostasy, i.e. leaving Islam. We noted that religious registration makes it clear who is classified before the law as a Muslim, and contrasted that with the self-identification element of those stating that they are not practising Muslims now. We also noted that in several cases people being accused of apostasy argued that they had never been practising Muslims. In Saudi Arabia we noted some citizens asking to be identified as atheists. Have such people left Islam? Are they to be regarded as apostates?

We noted in chapter 27 that apostasy should not be a crime. We can add here the observation that apostasy charges are rarely applied, even in those countries where they have been formally included in the Penal Code. Such practices undermine the concept of the clear rule of law applied equally to all. Is this theme of the Arab Awakening subtly challenging apostasy as a crime? Have societies throughout the Middle East come to realise this yet?

We can ask whether apostasy would be better viewed as a social and cultural measure of who has chosen to no longer be part of a Muslim community to which they once belonged. The Qur'an is clear that it is each individual who must answer before God for their actions and choices. One reference for this is Sura 6:164.

Many Muslims, some would argue most, reject any coercion in religion. In chapter 18 we noted that Daesh (who call themselves 'The Islamic State') forced some people to become like them, or at least to state that they had done so.

Authority within Islam is a major challenge, as it is in Judaism and Christianity. Appendix 3 gives some of the reasons for this.

The other issue we have noted at several points is the delicate, and not always obvious, balance of power between political and religious leaders in several states. In Iran we noted that in 2009 some citizens regarded their government as not truly Islamic, reflecting their dissatisfaction with how the authorities interpreted and applied Islamic teaching to the governance of the country.

One question that the truly religious need to ask is whether the benefits and costs of being the state religion enhance or hinder the religion's aspirations to inform and influence the beliefs, practice, attitudes and behaviours of its adherents? Muslims and Christians would also welcome the opportunity of inviting non-adherents to consider the claims of the religion and decide whether they wish to become followers.

This prompts a return to the topic of mobility within society. In chapter 4 we noted that religious registration emerged in a context of far less social mobility than is the case today. In chapter 10 we noted briefly that rising urbanisation is one of the factors profoundly affecting the Middle East. Mobility affects the communities of which individuals and families are a part. Does religious registration help or hinder communities as they say farewell to those moving elsewhere and welcome those moving in?

We need to be clear that using religious rites to mark key moments in life is desirable. So being able to use religiously based rites for marriage, to celebrate the birth of children and for burial is desired by many and by adherents of all faiths. What those of no faith, those whose religious registration is disputed – such as Meriam (chapter 11) and 300,000 Israelis (chapter 14) – and those people who choose marriage partners with different religious registrations appear to desire is a civil personal status code to complement – but not replace – religiously-based systems.

One of the many trends in the Arab Awakening is the increasing prevalence of generational issues. The question about the effect of religious registration on society seems even more pertinent here. It would appear that younger generations will increasingly adopt different methods of choosing marriage partners than did previous generations; relationship will be favoured over arrangement and the issue of keeping wealth within the clan will assume a lower priority. The August 2014 marriage in Israel of a Jewish lady with an Arab man is an example of a cross-community marriage. We noted that Sunni-Shi'a marriages were common in Baghdad prior to 2003. It seems likely that inter-community marriages will become more frequent in more places. Religious registration tends to restrict such a practice. Consequently, pressure will increase to add civil procedures to complement the religious practices. Where such diversity is respected, embraced and celebrated then the creative energy released seems likely to benefit society in many ways, as Marwan Muasher noted in his book whose title includes *The Battle for Pluralism and the Battle for Pluralism.*

One challenge within Judaism, Christianity and Islam is the spread of religious practice from the nominal to the devout. One clear articulation of this spectrum is in Israel. The Israeli Bureau of Statistics occasionally releases figures stating what proportion of Israeli Jews follow which school of Judaism. Of note is that approximately half are classified as 'secular Jews.' Such people do not attend worship on a regular basis. However, they do mark the national holidays that are based on Judaism's festivals. They are Jewish but not adherents of Judaism; they recognise that Judaism has shaped the culture, but not their own religious practice. Similar patterns are seen in Christian and Muslim communities. Religious registration masks such distinctions. It does not identify actual adherents or quantify how many people practise which faiths.

Another Arab Awakening theme is the need for more and better jobs. Again, does religious registration assist or hinder this? Does it facilitate harmonious working of diverse people? This merits exploring in both the private and public sectors. A sustained rapid expansion of private sector enterprise and employment seems to be essential to fulfil the desires being expressed.

Public sector employment in many Middle Eastern countries includes people from all faith backgrounds. However, discrimination based on religious registration is all too common for senior roles. There are 'glass ceilings' in all too many places.[43] Is one underlying assumption that those of other faiths are disloyal to the state? The vast majority of Christians in

[43] By glass ceiling we mean that promotion beyond a certain level is denied to some based on ethnic, religious, gender or other discriminatory grounds.

the Middle East utterly reject such a notion, stating that there is no factual basis for it. The same applies to other groups. True pluralism would not make such a presumption of disloyalty. We should also note that such issues apply on an intra-Muslim level too. One clear example concerns Shi'a in Saudi Arabia; similar issues apply in numerous countries. A positive example that we noted is the Druze community in Israel being affirmed as loyal citizens (chapter 14).

The removal of glass ceilings in public employment is something over which governments have full control. It could be one indicator of the progress towards greater pluralism. In chapter 10 we noted that this is equivalent to greater respect for diversity and greater encouragement of creativity. Consequently, there would be benefits within the private sector as creativity blossomed.

In chapter 12 we described the case of lay church leader Hamid Pourmand in Iran who was sentenced to three years' imprisonment in Iran for supposedly deceiving the army about his conversion to Christianity. Recall that Hamid presented evidence to the court that the authorities knew of his choice when they promoted him. From Hamid's perspective, the authorities promoted him on merit, and his Christian faith only became an issue when exposed for other reasons. This indicates that his loyalty to the state was not in question, and that his competency was affirmed, respected and rewarded. Is religious registration helping governments ensure that administrative functions are carried out with the highest degree of professionalism possible for the benefit of the whole society?

Private sector employment is a more mixed picture. In Egypt and Jordan, Christians own a disproportionately high number of businesses with the consequence that discrimination in private sector employment tends to favour rather than disadvantage Christians. This is a national average and there are local variations. The same is not true in other countries. For example, we noted that in Turkey one reason why some of those who convert to Christianity do not change their religious registration is to avoid adverse discrimination in employment.

The distinction between public and private sector is not always clear. In several countries a number of businesses are owned or controlled by the military or other government bodies. Official statistics are not available, although it is commonly understood that in Egypt approximately 40% of economic activity is effectively within the public sector while for Iran the estimate is 70%. Discrimination in public sector employment can be more wide ranging than it appears.

It is worth noting that one critical factor in the early history and flourishing of the Arab Empire in the seventh century was that it created a context for equitable trading both within its own territory and with neighbouring areas (see appendix 3). There are several economic powerhouses within the Arab world, notably in the Gulf states. I trust that this is an encouragement that more places throughout the Arab world can become locations with high quality jobs.

In chapter 10 we described the prevalence of patronage in societies across the Middle East. This is the concept that individuals look for a patron who provides them with resources and opportunities in exchange for loyalty. What is required is that more people start looking to create such opportunities for themselves in seeking employment or starting their own businesses. The latter gives such entrepreneurs the possibility of becoming patrons for others.

A related theme is the pressure for the clear rule of law applied equally to all. This is a prerequisite for inward economic investment in an increasingly interconnected world. Businesses need to know that contracts they sign will be honoured and can be enforced if necessary. They do not desire or need the distraction of legal processes, but they do need the reassurance that terms and conditions for suppliers and customers can be enforced, and any disputes settled legally if necessary. The implications for private sector employment are clear, i.e. the clear rule of national law is a prerequisite for the creation of more and better jobs.

The clear rule of law applied equally to all affects all aspects of society. Might it be possible to address employment issues by concentrating on good legal frameworks and enforcement of contracts and other aspects of law of direct relevance to business and commerce? If the answer is 'yes,' surely there would be wider benefits across society as a whole. We noted during our regional tour the effects of inconsistent legal decisions in Jordan, Egypt and Saudi Arabia. The resulting uncertainty is not helpful. In Saudi Arabia our focus was on the business community asking for clarity. In Jordan and Egypt our specific focus was on inconsistent application to those recognised as Christians. The desire is for all to be treated as citizens first and adherents of a particular faith second.

We conclude these reflections on creating employment and promoting dynamic economies by asking whether religious registration helps or hinders? Discrimination of any sort is rarely helpful.

The Arab Awakening appears to be pressing for more equitable electoral systems. This would suggest ending the religiously-based elements, including designated parliamentary seats for ethnic or religious groups. We noted that in Jordan and Lebanon such allocations over-represent Christians, and that in Lebanon it is typically Christian leaders who are resistant to changes to the electoral system. In contrast, the designation of seats in Egypt and Iraq appears to be tokenistic. Egypt is changing, and appears likely to continue to do so. Pope Tawadros' encouragement of Egyptian Christians to become more actively involved in politics is a call for a more pluralistic approach, where diversity of view and contribution is seen as strengthening the whole community.

We noted in chapter 18 the example of Kirkuk's incumbent mayor attracting votes from all the ethnic groups in recognition of his competence and governance for the benefit of all. In this case, the governance style came first and precipitated the cross-ethnic voting. We can hope that such practice becomes widespread.

Algeria's ethnic diversity is clear; there are several Berber ethnicities present, of which the Kabyle are the most numerous. In contrast, what do we understand by the statement in its constitution that all citizens are Muslim? We noted earlier that there is some element of recognition for Algerian churches, an acknowledgement that not all Algerians are Muslims. So why does the constitution state what is manifestly not true? Is anyone being deceived? What effect does this have on the establishment of the clear rule of law applied equally to all?

One of Morocco's quiet reforms has been to give greater recognition to ethnic groups, notably by use of their languages. Constitutional amendments made in 2011 included making Tamazight, a Berber language spoken by an estimated 40% of Moroccans, an official language alongside Arabic. Can we view this as an example of welcoming and embracing diversity, of addressing the pluralism deficit? Can we observe, together with the Moroccan people, how this affects society? Might it improve the clear rule of law applied to all? Will it lead to greater creativity with consequent economic benefit in the form of more and better jobs?

One theme we have noted at several points is the balance between national and religious law, especially when the two clash. To some, this can be viewed as the balance between man's authority and God's authority. The challenge that needs to be faced is how society should be structured and managed to reflect and respect its ethnic and religious diversity so that it can flourish for the benefit of everyone. In most matters, religious law is welcomed where its authority is genuinely respected and desired by all parties to the matters in hand. The difficulties occur where one or more parties desire either a different religiously-based system or a civil alternative. The religious registration systems prevalent in the Middle East today sometimes force the use of specific religious courts on people. Is this helpful?

The Arab Awakening is, amongst other things, a cry for citizenship; for the dignity of all, for the clear rule of law applied equally to all, irrespective of their place in society. Consequently, the Arab Awakening is challenging how the religious registration systems are applied.

Conclusion

Christians in the Middle East are asking, "Help us find a way through" – that is through the effects on individuals, communities and society of the current use of religious registration systems. Our journey through the region has shown the myriad challenges that are encountered.

The stories of individuals have illustrated the range of problems in the area of personal status law. Martha in Egypt is an example of someone unable to legally marry the man she loved. In Israel we noted that a large number of people were unable to get married in their own country. The same applies in Egypt, whose government also refuses to recognise the validity of marriages contracted abroad if the marriage would not be allowed under the country's religiously-based system. We noted too that the law obliges a man to switch his registration to Muslim if he wishes to marry a woman registered as a Muslim.

Religious registration can lead to battles over custody of children, as Siham, Ramzi and Muna (Jordan), Martha and the twins (Egypt) discovered. In such battles, meeting the needs of the children is significant by its absence. Consequences for parents include being forced to live in hiding as did Martha together with her family or having to leave their country as did Ramzi and Muna. Uğur's story (Turkey) illustrates that some are buried using rites from a faith that they no longer adhere to.

Ramzi and Muna felt obliged to leave their country because of the challenge posed by the religious registration system. This is in sharp contrast with calls by political and religious leaders for Christians to remain, a recognition and affirmation that they are valued members of society. Yet, discrimination on religious grounds in employment remains prevalent, with the presence of glass ceilings in public sector employment being an example of the lack of trust that Christians and members of other communities are truly loyal citizens. The difference between pronouncement and practice is palpable.

Demiana (Egypt) also chose to leave her country when the legal system failed to clear her of accusations of wrongdoing that had clearly been shown to be false. Such injustice within the legal system is symptomatic of Christians being treated as second-class citizens, a practice underpinned by religious registration.

Religious registration creates a crisis of identity for those who choose to become Christians, primarily due to the reaction of those in their communities. Most converts strongly desire to remain loyal to their family, community and country. The typical pattern is that immediate family members come to accept and respect their change of religious belief and practice. Where serious problems arise they are usually initiated by members of the wider family. Ramzi and Muna's story fits with this pattern.

In some cases it is the authorities that initiate action against converts. We looked at stories from Jordan (a family whose religious registration was changed based on events 40 years previously) and Egypt (a senior judge asking the Constitutional Court whether the Supreme Administration Court's decision about reconverts was constitutional). The governments of North African and Arabian Peninsula countries treat all citizens as though they are Muslims even when they know that this is not the case. For example, Algeria has granted recognition to a national church body and Saudi Arabia's government will be only too aware of the calls by some Saudis to be recognised as atheists.

The experiences of Mohammed Hegazy (Egypt), pastor Yousef (Iran) and Meriam (Sudan) demonstrate that religious registration is not, in essence, about religious belief or practice. Mohammed was told that he would not be allowed to change his registration irrespective of his beliefs. This reduces religion to a social control mechanism, undermining the essence of religion as being an exploration, alone and with others, of the relationship between the natural and supernatural realms of reality and the individual's place within each realm.

Case studies have shown what happens to some Christians. Such challenges can emerge unexpectedly, as happened to Ramzi and Muna (Jordan), Demiana (Egypt), Meriam and her family (Sudan) and Hamid Pourmand (Iran). Many Christians throughout the Middle East live with the awareness that they, or those close to them, might be the next victims of religiously motivated injustice of which religious registration is a major contributing element.

For church leaders, a typical challenge is how to respond to requests for assistance from those whose religious registration is not Christian. They fear repercussions should they be seen to be welcoming non-Christians into church buildings or events. They are very careful in responding to the question of 'may I worship with you?'

Religious registration has subtle effects on some communities. Druze communities in Lebanon appreciate being able to conduct personal status matters according to their own customs and rites. They are an example where religion and ethnic identity merge. Most Lebanese Druze who convert to Christianity leave their religious registration as Druze, regarding it as primarily an ethnic identification, not a religious one. Ethnically Jewish Israeli citizens who choose to become Christians likewise retain their allegiance to their ethnicity whilst becoming adherents of a different religion. They do not have the option of changing which religiously-based system of personal status law applies to them; some are denied marriages within their own country.

We can summarise the problems by stating that religious registration creates a myriad set of challenges for individuals, religious institutions and society. The violation of the rights of individuals contravenes accepted international norms, in whose establishment an Arab, Charles Malik, played a leading role. Society is harmed as reduced respect for diversity lessens economic activity to the detriment of all. The overt segregation of society on religious lines contributes to a context in which overt identification of the 'other' facilitates discrimination and contributes to a context conducive to the perpetration of acts of violence. Religious registration is symptomatic of the pluralism deficit and a significant contributor to it.

We noted that violence occurs both as local sectarian clashes as seen in Egypt and also as widespread conflicts as seen in Iraq, Syria, Yemen and elsewhere.

The macro level context of the Middle East shows most countries struggling to adapt to meet the rising aspirations of their people as expressed in the Arab Awakening. All countries need to adapt and some are doing so. Many people across the Middle East are calling for greater dignity and broader opportunities. They desire to be treated as citizens, equal before the law irrespective of ethnicity, gender, social background, education level or religious identification. They want to be part of a flourishing society, one that respects and cherishes diversity as a creative force that supports the wellbeing of all. Addressing the pluralism deficit is one action that would assist in realising their aspirations.

It is clear that the Arab Awakening is not a call for religion to be removed from society or public debate. Egyptians in Tahrir Square in 2011 desired to pray, and Muslims and Christians enabled one another to do so. The call is for religious views to inform public debate and for mutual respect amongst adherents of different faiths and different strands of the same faith, as well as those of no faith.

The last chapter concluded with the observation that the Arab Awakening is challenging the assumptions and application of religious registration systems in many countries in the Middle East, although it is not clear how widely this is recognised.

"Help us find a way through." What are the potential solutions to these challenges?

At the macro level we have seen two clear calls for pluralistic approaches to be adopted, namely Egypt's President Sisi (chapter 10) and the National Dialogue process in Yemen (chapter 22). Such initiatives are to be encouraged. A pertinent component needs to be the clear rule of law applied equally to all. It is worth keeping in mind that one reason that Islam spread rapidly immediately after its founding was that it created an environment in which equitable trading could flourish.

Many of the personal status issues would be addressed by creating a civil system to complement existing religiously based systems. This would cater for all those unable or unwilling to use the religiously based systems that are their only option at present. This would facilitate the recognition of marriages properly contracted abroad, a practice that Israel and Lebanon follow but Egypt in particular does not.

For the specifically religious aspects, some converts are asking for the right to change their religious registration to match their beliefs. At present, Turkish law makes this a simple process in which the individual chooses from the list of allowed registrations and Lebanese law requires a letter of welcome from the millet (see Glossary) that an individual wishes to join. Atheists in several countries are asking to be recognised as such. How they regard their religious registration is unclear. The obvious assumption is that they would like the option of civil marriage procedures and their being the option for officially recognising their chosen belief.

Lawsuits have occurred challenging the restrictions that prevent some being able to change their religious registration to match their chosen beliefs. At some point the Mohammed Hegazy case in Egypt will be resumed: Egyptian society needs to know what is meant by freedom of belief being an absolute right. Other countries in the Middle East will be obliged to confront the same challenge. It is clear to some that this topic is part of the discussion of the future nature of society and whether or not society as a whole will flourish for the benefit of all.

Apostasy (i.e. leaving Islam) should not be a crime, whilst recognising that there are often social costs for those who convert, many of whom become devout adherents of one religion having been nominal in religious practice while part of another religiously based community.

During our regional tour we observed several serious problems in a number of countries. In Egypt in numerous crimes involving Christians the initial police investigations were handled poorly. The story of Demiana (chapter 9) illustrates that evidence is not accurately assessed in an impartial manner during certain court cases. In Iran religious activities by Christians are treated as anti-state actions despite

Iranian Christians being loyal citizens. The same is true of Turkey's Christians. In Jordan Shari'a courts are able to annul all the rights of citizens. One approach would be to limit the jurisdiction of religious courts to those willing to submit to their authority. In Saudi Arabia the legal framework generates uncertainty caused by varying interpretations of Shari'a causing a lack of clarity to those seeking to live, work and worship in an honourable manner.

One theme in all these specific issues is the acceptance that people different from the 'majority' are accepted as valued citizens. Society would benefit if the cultural norm moved towards diversity being welcomed as enriching the whole; the pluralism deficit needs addressing. One step towards this would be the overt recognition that people of goodwill who desire the flourishing of society for the mutual benefit of all constitute the large majority of people. Furthermore, this majority is multi-religious in most societies as well as multi-ethnic in many. One tangible step for national governments would be to end glass ceilings in public employment. Another would be to ensure that justice is done as assessed by law rather than notions of what is honourable or shameful. Within the prevailing honour-shame culture it needs to become the norm that honourable behaviour respects diversity and it is shameful to make false accusations or for officials to ignore some evidence or the outcome of independent investigations.

A challenging element of this cultural change is the need to recognise that an individual can choose to become an adherent of a different faith whilst remaining loyal to and supportive of their family, community and country. A further element is the recognition that there is a distinction between being a Muslim on paper and being someone with Islamic religious beliefs and practices.

Those countries across North Africa and the Arabian Peninsula that regard all citizens as Muslims need to review their understanding of what that means. Many do not treat all Muslims as equal, typically marginalising the adherents of Shi'a Islam. Some citizens have chosen to become adherents of other faiths and some are calling to be recognised as atheists.

The Middle East and the broader Arab world is a complex region with a rich and diverse history and culture. This region has flourished in the past; parts of it flourish today; and more of it is well able to flourish in the future providing the leadership at local, provincial and national levels creates a suitable context. Religious leaders from all faiths should consider whether they are part of the problem or part of the solution and work to create societies where all communities can flourish – even if that involves their surrendering some of their perceived position, privileges and power. What contribution would they like to make in order to reduce the pluralism deficit? If society as a whole flourishes then so will the local communities of which they are a part.

I trust that this book assists the people of the region find a way through the challenges of religious registration. I hope it will encourage people in other parts of the world to understand and engage with what is happening in the Middle East. I long that together we can be part of a flourishing and diverse future.

Appendix 1

A brief history of Judaism in the Middle East

In chapter 14 we noted that Israel has two Chief Rabbis, one each for Ashkenazi and Sephardi Judaism, and we used the terms Haredim and Ultra-Orthodox. We also mentioned Karaite and Reform Judaism. From where do these strands within Judaism today originate?

The following is a brief history, seeking to illustrate the origins of these terms and the diversity that we see today. More detailed treatments of the history are available elsewhere. Similarly, the following two appendices are summaries of the origins of the diversity within Christianity and Islam in the Middle East.

We could summarise the defining points of the history recorded in the Hebrew scriptures (known to Christians as the Old Testament) as the call of Abraham, the move to Egypt led by Joseph, the exodus from Egypt led by Moses, the establishment of the kingdom of Israel with Joshua, Samuel, David and Solomon as key characters, the split of the kingdom that followed, the exile to Babylon and the restoration to Jerusalem and a small surrounding area.

The Babylonian exile proved to be a significant period. Much of the Jewish canon was finalised during this period and new patterns of worship were devised. All forms of worship in Judaism trace their origins to this period, although the current written formulations date from much later periods. Sephardi and Ashkenazi are different liturgical patterns of worship.

The teachings of Judaism were initially primarily oral, although written versions have existed for millennia. Some have been gathered together into what is known as the Talmud. One component, the Mishnah, dates from around the year 200 CE. A second component, the Gemara, dates from approximately 500 CE and is a collection of Rabbinic writings. The term *Talmud* can be used to mean either the Gemara alone or the Mishnah and Gemara together. The tradition of Rabbinic teaching produced the Talmud. The Talmud is a revered text, with some ascribing it sacred text status.

Under the Roman Empire the Jews were a protected ethnic-religious group and there were flourishing Jewish communities in many places. The Septuagint, i.e. the Greek language translation of the Old Testament and some related texts, was produced in Alexandria in the second century BCE. The name refers to the fact that the work was undertaken by 70 scholars. This made the

Hebrew scriptures available in the common trade language of the Empire.

Karaite Judaism accepts only the Torah as a definite sacred text, i.e. the Talmud and Mishnah are not accepted as definitive. The Karaite community emphasises reading the Torah only (the first five books of the Hebrew Scriptures, often attributed to Moses), looking for the most natural meaning for the original recipients and interpreting that understanding as simply as possible for today. It traces its history to the seventh century. It is generally accepted as being formalised in Baghdad, although similar ideas may have emerged independently in Egypt. There are similarities, but also crucial differences, to the views of the Sadducees, a strand prominent in the first century.

Sephardi Judaism's liturgy emerged in the Iberian Peninsula - modern day Spain and Portugal - around the end of the first millennium. This community flourished until the Alhambra Decree, also known as the Edict of Expulsion, was issued by Spain's Monarchs on 31st March 1492. This ordered all Jews to leave their territories by 31st July 1492 and led to many Iberian Jews migrating, as well as forced conversions and executions of those who chose to stay or were unable to leave. The Decree was formally rescinded by the Second Vatican Council in 1962. The displaced took their patterns of worship with them. We need to note that the term Sephardi today can be used in a narrow sense to mean those descended from Iberian Peninsula Jews and in a broader sense to mean those who follow the form of worship that emerged there. Such people trace their more recent ancestry to Jews in Asia and elsewhere, as well as the Iberian Peninsula.

Ashkenazi Judaism's liturgy emerged in Central and Western Europe. The current formulations can only be traced in literary forms to the early medieval period, although their development goes back to previous eras.

Haredi Judaism emerged as a response to modernity. This community regards itself as the most authentic community within Judaism, a claim that is disputed by other streams. The Haredim segregate themselves from secular society, hence their insistence within Israel on operating their own schools. They take the study of scripture very seriously, with their name literally meaning 'one who trembles at the word of God', derived from Isaiah 66:2,5. The term ultra-Orthodox is generally synonymous with the Haredi. However, its usage is declining due to it being regarded by some as a derogatory term expressing extremism.

During the Ottoman Empire era the Jews were a defined millet. At some times they were a respected minority who flourished; at other times they were persecuted. In general, they fared better in the Middle East than in much of Europe, which prompted some Jewish people to migrate to the Empire from Europe.

In the nineteenth and twentieth centuries a new form of Judaism arose, often referred to as Reform Judaism or the Progressive Movement. This form of Judaism subjected Jewish law to a critical review or reform in order that adherents could live appropriately in the modern age within their communities. This form of Judaism originated in the USA and was established in Israel in the 1970s, where it is known as the Israeli Progressive Movement, often shortened to Reform.

What unites Judaism, and indeed the Jewish people, is a shared story which includes numerous displacements, becoming settled in a new place and then exiled again. The desire for a full return and a permanent, enduring, even eternal, residence in a specific place is a recurring theme. Until such a hope is realised, one crucial theological question is how to live and worship as a diaspora.

Appendix 2

A brief history of Christianity in the Middle East

This is a brief summary of the history, seeking to illustrate the origins of some of the diverse range of Churches that exist in the Middle East today.

Christianity itself originated in the Middle East. Jesus Christ was born in Bethlehem, was crucified and rose in Jerusalem and ascended to heaven. The Church was founded fifty days after the resurrection on the day of Pentecost, also in Jerusalem.

Christ's followers, i.e. Christians, spread out from Jerusalem in all directions, founding numerous groups of adherents in a wide variety of places. The young Church of the first century knew periods of quiet acceptance and periods of intense persecution. The Acts of the Apostles, the fifth book of the New Testament (part of the Christian Bible) gives a partial picture, focusing on the westward spread towards Rome. This pattern continued until AD 295 when Christianity was declared the official religion of the Roman Empire.

Christianity remained the state religion as the Roman Empire split into the Byzantine Empire and the Holy

Roman Empire. During this period the Christian faith was spread to other areas by missionaries.

By the fifth century there was a significant part of the church that lived under the Persian Empire. Due to the enmity between the Byzantine and Persian empires the situation of the church in the Persian areas was precarious. Christianity was the state religion in the Byzantine Empire and so Persian Christians were perceived as either disloyal or as potentially disloyal to their political rulers.

At the Council of Ephesus held in AD 431 the Christological ideas ascribed to Nestorius were condemned. (It is debatable whether Nestorius was a Nestorian! The views of many active theologians at this time are only known through their opponents, who were not necessarily the most accurate or generous in their assessments.) Seeing a chance to distance the church in the Persian Empire from the Byzantine Church, the Persian Christians supported the followers of the views that were condemned at the council. This led to the formation of the Assyrian Church of the East. This church does not accept any Ecumenical Council other than the first, namely the Council of Nicea held in AD 325 at which the Nicene Creed was adopted as a succinct summary of Christian belief. While the Assyrian Church of the East has a form of the Eastern-rite liturgy it is not in communion with either the Oriental Orthodox or Eastern Orthodox churches. The formation of this church used a theological issue as cover for an underlying political motivation of demonstrating to their rulers that they were different from the state church of the Byzantine Empire that was in competition with the Persian Empire. They were loyal citizens, as well as Christians.

The next schism happened at the Council of Chalcedon held in AD 451. The council reached consensus on a certain Christological definition of the relationship between the two natures of Jesus Christ, i.e. fully divine and fully human. For many reasons local Christians in certain areas of the Middle East and Central Asia did not agree and refused the conclusions of the Council. They became known as the Oriental Orthodox Churches. They are also known as Miaphysite (or Monophysite) Churches, or the non-Chalcedonian Orthodox Churches (which somewhat unkindly defines them by what they are not). Within the Middle East the main members of this family of churches are the Coptic Orthodox Church in areas that are now part of Egypt and the Horn of Africa, the Syriac Orthodox Church in the Levant and the Armenian Apostolic Church which is concentrated in present-day Armenia and Central Asia. These groups split from the Byzantine state church.

The next big schism is commonly dated as occurring in 1054. It would be more accurate to say that a significant step in a long process occurred in that year. The main question was the primacy of the conflict between the "Western" church with the most important episcopal see (or bishop) in Rome and the "Eastern" church. They cannot be termed different churches because at that time they remained part of the one Byzantine church. There were many differences between them, including philosophical and theological issues, and claims over which episcopal see was the more important. The church split into two: the "Western" church, which chose the Bishop of Rome as it leader and became known as the Catholic Church, and the church of the East, which chose the Bishop of Constantinople as the most prominent church leader (not as a 'Pope' in the Catholic sense, but as a 'primus inter pares,' a first amongst equals) and became known as the Eastern Orthodox Church.

The "Filioque" clause in the Nicene Creed has become a useful theological label for the schism, although it appears to have not been so significant at the time. The Filioque clause is the phrase "and the Son" added to the Spirit's emanating from the Father. The Western churches typically include this whereas the Eastern churches do not.

The next major development in the history of the Church in the Middle East was the period of the Crusades, 1095-1291. These were a period of much violence, plunder and territorial conquest. There was an intra-Christendom element in addition to the Christian versus Jew and Muslim elements, notably when Constantinople was attacked during the Fourth Crusade. One consequence concerning church traditions was to split several of the Orthodox churches to create a Catholic equivalent loyal to Rome rather than the Orthodox structures. An example of a denomination that emerged in this way is the Syrian Catholic.

The next major development within Christendom happened in Europe when the Reformation split the Western church into Catholic and Protestant traditions. This process is often dated as starting in 1517 and concluding in 1648 with the Peace of Westphalia. The process may have started with theological concerns documented by Martin Luther but it had numerous factors including nationalism, the rise of humanism and the place of reason in religion.

The last major development in the Middle East was the arrival of Protestant denominations from the nineteenth century onwards. Many of these are the result of Western missionary activity; Henry Martyn (1781-1812) was one of the early practitioners and is credited with an early translation of the New Testament into Farsi, the primary language of Iran. In some cases, the new arrivals endeavoured to work with indigenous churches before deciding to create new churches whose names are derived from the Western denominations. In many cases these new Protestant churches attracted indigenous believers to become members and slowly became authentic local churches rather than Western implants. There are lingering tensions in some countries between these Protestant denominations and the longer-established Orthodox and Catholic churches.

Appendix 3

A brief history of Islam in the Middle East

As with the previous two appendices, the intention here is to give an indication of the origins of the numerous Islamic traditions and communities within the Middle East. It does not attempt to be a comprehensive historical account.

The traditional view of the founding of Islam is that it originates in the life of the prophet Muhammad, who was born in approximately 570 and died in 632. (There are alternative views discussed in some theological circles within Islam, but such discussions are rarely seen elsewhere and are not our concern.) Islam emerged as a unifying force on the Arabian Peninsula, an area that previously only had language in common. It emerged in a context that knew only oral Jewish and Christian teaching and traditions, a fact that probably underlies the inaccurate and misquoted statements of Christian doctrine found in the Qur'an, Islam's sacred text, and other early Islamic writings.

One immediate effect was to create a context for equitable trade amongst the various groups scattered over the Arabian Peninsula, and subsequently for trade networks with Africa's east coast and India's west coast. The presence in Oman of citizens whose mother tongue is Swahili is a legacy of such trade.

Upon Muhammad's death, the Muslim community debated who should succeed him as their leader, carrying the title of Caliph. Two schools of thought rapidly emerged, either that leadership should pass to the direct descendants of the prophet or that the community as a whole should choose.

This debate prompted the first schism within Islam. Those who favoured ancestral succession became known as Shi'a. The name, literally 'The Party of Ali,' is derived from the cousin and son-in-law of Muhammad. Those who took the alternative view of the community choosing their leader became known as Sunnis. The term 'Sunni' is derived from Sunna meaning the habitual practice of Muhammad with the literal meaning of 'as-Sunna' (the Sunna) being 'people of the path.'

Tensions came to a head in 656 when the third leader after Muhammad, Caliph Uthman, was murdered, suffering the same fate as his two predecessors. By this time the Arab and Muslim community had greatly expanded the area under its control. A struggle for succession ensued between Ali, cousin and son-in-law of Muhammad, and Mu'awiyah, the governor of Syria and cousin of Uthman. Supporters of the two men met in battle in 657. This battle proved inconclusive, with both men agreeing to arbitration, a decision that proved controversial. One consequence was the formation of the Kharijite movement, some of whose members assassinated Ali in 661, ostensibly because he had made compromises with a rival Muslim faction. The Kharijite movement is widely perceived to be heretical within Islam. Peace was agreed and Mu'awiyah was accepted as the next Caliph. However, his death in 680 led to a further civil war. In the same year, Ali's son Hussein was killed by an Arab army in a battle at Karbala, in modern day Iraq. Hussein had married a Persian lady with one consequence being the addition of an Arab-Persian dynamic to the struggle. These events formalised the split between Sunni and Shi'a within Islam.

The time of these first Caliphs is regarded as a golden age by some within the Muslim community. They aspire to re-enact that period when the religious and political leadership was combined and territorial expansion was rapid. The new rulers were often welcomed as an improvement on the local leadership that they had displaced.

Shari'a is often termed as Islamic jurisprudence, although this designation limits its scope in the eyes of some. Shari'a covers the whole of life, i.e. it informs criminal, civil and personal legal codes, as well as addressing issues of daily life and personal and corporate prayer. The term literally means 'the way' and so can be understood as being the Islamic way of doing things, all things.

There are a variety of interpretations of Shari'a. Over time these have been written down and the differences noted. Today there are five Medhabs or 'schools' of Shari'a, one within Shi'a Islam, the Ja'afari school, and four within Sunni Islam, namely the Hanafi, Hanbali, Maliki and Shafi'i. A sixth school, the Jariri, emerged within Sunni Islam but subsequently died out. Each school has variations within it. The Maliki school is referred to as the Zahiri school in some sources. The four Sunni schools were established in the eighth and ninth centuries based on the writings of their founders; all four of whom accepted the legitimacy of the others, and encouraged Sunnis to adopt whichever school they wished to abide by. The Medhabs have been modified over the centuries, such as in regard to slavery, which was prevalent in most societies in the eighth century, has been allowed to lapse based on consensus.

Over time, different 'groupings' emerged within both Sunni and Shi'a Islam, and there are some Islamic traditions that are neither Sunni nor Shi'a. The major groupings within Shi'a Islam are the Ja'afari also known as the 'Twelver,' and the Ismaili, sometimes called the 'Sevener.' Another group is the Zaidi, which is closer in many respects to Sunni Islam than other forms of Shi'a Islam. Zaidi is sometimes referred to as 'Fiver.'

One group not within Sunni or Shi'a is Ibadhi Islam. This emerged in the tenth century, as a revival of the Kharijite movement of early Islamic history. The Kharijite, literally *withdrawers*, emphasised a puritanical, rural lifestyle based on the belief that simply being a Muslim was insufficient to get to heaven. They advocated appropriate lifestyle as an additional requirement, i.e. the faith must be lived as well as believed. Today, Ibadhi Islam sees itself as distinct from the Kharijite movement. It is characterised by detailed points about how to pray and the belief that one can lose salvation by committing a major sin. Ibadhi Islam is the predominant faith in Oman and there are a small number of adherents in Algeria and elsewhere.

The emergence of two further strands within Islam is worth consideration. Salafism is within Sunni Islam and can be traced back to Ibn Taymiyyah (1263-1328) who taught that Muslims should strive to return to the way of the companions of the Muhammad. His view can be understood as ignoring the Medhabs' interpretation of the earliest Islamic sources in favour of interpreting such sources directly. In Arabic, the word *salaf* means forefathers. Ibn Taymiyyah is also credited with establishing the practice of *takfir*, the declaring of Muslims deemed insufficiently Islamic as *kuffar*, or infidels.

Salafism is closely linked to Wahhabism which is named after Mohammed ibn 'Abd al-Wahhab (1703-1792), who called for a puritanical form of Islam, purged of all heresies and idolatry. He drew upon a number of previous Islamic thinkers including Ibn Taymiyyah. Al-Wahhab was forced to leave his home town, leading to a period of wandering before he found protection under the al-Saud clan in 1741. The al-Saud clan in Arabia used Wahhabi teachings to justify conquering and ruling neighbouring tribes. Their area of control expanded in the eighteenth and early nineteenth centuries but declined from 1812 to 1818 when they were steadily defeated as the Ottoman Empire reasserted its control. A revival of al-Saud fortunes in the 1920s led to the creation of Saudi Arabia under King Abd-al Aziz. Under this political control, Wahhabism within Saudi Arabia was pressured to become a conservative social, political and religious movement upholding loyalty to the ruling family and the monarch's absolute power.

Salafism can be regarded as having three approaches, sometimes termed 'quiet,' 'active' and 'jihadist.' The quiet approach emphasises teaching and proclamation of the faith. Activists pressure their governments to rule using Islamic principles. The jihadist approach is to engage in 'holy war.'

The second strand to consider is the Sufi movement which combines elements of orthodox Islam with various mystical practices. There are Sufi movements within Sunni and Shi'a Islam. The term Sufi is derived from the Arabic word *suf* meaning wool and reflects the ascetic practices of wearing simple woollen garments. Sufism emerged early in Islamic history and is an example of the combining of Islamic teaching with previous religious practices.

Such syncretism led to the emergence of strands within Islam whose status is disputed. One such is the Alawite, who are accepted as part of Shi'a Islam by some and regarded as heretical by others. Another are the Alevi, who some regard as part of Shi'a Islam and some prefer to regard as a distinct faith, outside the house of Islam.

In addition there are post-Islamic faiths, belief systems that emerged after Islam and include some elements derived from earlier faiths. The Baha'i is one such faith, which gladly accepts being a distinct religion. Their worldwide headquarters are in Haifa, Israel. They emerged in the nineteenth century and draw on the sacred texts of all previous faiths as well as the teachings of their founder Baha'u'llah. Central to their beliefs are the unity of God, the unity of mankind and the unity of religions. They are widely condemned within Islamic communities, in essence because they deny that Muhammad was the final prophet sent by God, the final act of divine revelation.

The traditional narrative of the founding of Islam combines political and spiritual leadership. Critics often observe that violence is present from the earliest period. Proponents point out that the territorial expansion was rapid because it was widely welcomed. Crucial in the earliest history was the establishment of equitable trading, an observation that is pertinent to the present calls for more and better jobs. The intra-Islam violence seen today is one cause of an identity crisis amongst some Muslims; the violence and inhumanity overtly claimed in the name of the religion appals them, causing some to question their Muslim identity.

Appendix 4

A brief history of the Middle East in the twentieth century

This appendix is intended to give an overview of the major political developments that shaped the Middle East during the twentieth century. It is a big picture type overview, summarising in a few pages what could be a book in itself.

The twentieth century began with the Ottoman Empire in control of much of the Middle East and beyond. Its control of North Africa was already lessening, with many areas effectively governing themselves with large degrees of autonomy.

The end of the First World War saw the start of a period of Western colonial rule of much of the region. Most of the current nation states were formed during this period. Two documents proved crucial during this process, namely the Sykes-Picot Agreement of 1916 and the Balfour Declaration of 1917. The former detailed the agreement between the UK and France on the respective areas that they would control in what became Iraq, Israel, Jordan, Lebanon, Palestine and Syria. The latter committed the UK government to the creation of a state for Jewish people in the Middle East.

The majority of states are colonial constructs. One clear exception is Egypt, which has a long history and hence a cohesive sense of national identity within its borders. This is arguably also the case for Tunisia, which is one reason why it has handled the Arab Awakening in a more cohesive manner than countries such as Libya and Syria. Saudi Arabia is a construct, but one made by the Al-Saud family who succeeded in uniting a disparate group of tribes under the religious leadership of Wahhabi clerics and the political leadership of their family.

Many of the states created by the West were inherently unstable and several endured one or more coups which led to one-party dictatorships. Examples of this are Egypt, Iraq, Sudan and Syria. Some of the states ruled by a monarchy have proved more stable, such as Jordan, Morocco and the small Gulf states. In contrast, the monarchies instituted in Egypt and Iraq proved short lived.

One major cause of instability in states that were colonial constructs was the lack of a cohesive sense of shared identity, which contributes to the sense of a crisis of identity felt by some, e.g. Iraq (see chapter 18).

Another factor was the history of being governed in a top-down, often heavy-handed manner as part of an empire. Local control of personal status was part of this history and continued into the modern era.

One common element in the Arab Awakening is the clear call by the people for involvement in their governance. This is challenging the history of empire and dictatorial governance that has prevailed for centuries.

Let us highlight a few years in which developments that were to prove significant occurred. In 1924 the recently formed state of Turkey cancelled the Caliphate. Under the Ottoman Empire, the Sultan was also the Caliph, the leader of all Muslims. In practice, the Caliph was a Sunni and few Shi'a acknowledged his claims to represent all Muslims. This development raised the question of who is the undisputed leader of the Muslim community as a whole. It remains unresolved.

In 1947 the UN issued a Partition Plan which divided what was referred to as Palestine into a Jewish state and a Palestinian state. The first Jew-Arab war of the twentieth century ensued. On 15th May 1948 the State of Israel was declared. Egypt assumed formal sovereignty for the Gaza Strip and Jordan for the West Bank. Such sovereignty has been dropped.

The Six Day War in June 1967 profoundly changed the regional dynamics, notably concerning the development of political Islam. We shall return to this after noting the events of 1979. This was the year that saw the Iranian revolution, Saddam Hussein became President of Iraq, the Camp David Accords established diplomatic relations between Egypt and Israel and the Soviets invaded Afghanistan, an event that was to affect the shape of political Islam, with global consequences.

One consequence of the Six Day War was the emergence of Palestinian militancy. In September 1970 three airliners were hijacked to Dawson Field in Jordan. The passengers were released but the aircraft were destroyed. (This incident has a personal significance to me; watching it on the news aged 12 prompted me to wonder why people behaved in such ways. It was the start of my study of Middle Eastern issues.) The Jordanian government responded by forcibly displacing a large number of Palestinians from their territory in an operation referred to as Black September. Many moved to Lebanon, where their presence disturbed the delicate balance of society and became one cause of the Lebanese civil war, which is commonly dated as 1975-1991.

Intertwined with the political history was the development of political Islam and the changing status of the Christian church within society. Islamic reform movements emerged during the sixteenth to eighteenth centuries, prompted by several notable thinkers including Abd al-Wahhab (1703-1792) in Arabia who founded what became known as Wahhabi Islam which is prevalent in Saudi Arabia and Qatar today. (See appendix 3) However, in the first half of the twentieth century such movements were not, in general, major players in events. Another reformist movement emerged in these years with Ali Abd al-Razeq (1888-1966) defending Turkey's abolition of the Caliphate in 1924 and the curriculum of al-Azhar being restructured. During this period, the Church continued much as before, with its legal status similar to that during the Ottoman Empire. The planning regulations governing church buildings in Egypt is an example.

A marked change occurred in 1967. Much of Arab society felt shamed by the defeat of Arab military forces in the Six Day War by a relative newcomer and non-Islamic entity. The phrase "Islam is the answer" started to be widely used together with calls for Shari'a law to be implemented. Both were used as rallying cries for political reforms and a more Islamic state. The Muslim Brotherhood became more prominent, the modern reformist movement dissipated and al-Azhar's curriculum changed. Several countries adjusted their constitutions, including Egypt in 1981, to add that Shari'a would be the principle source of legislation. What actual changes ensued is open to debate.

Militant Islam with a global agenda emerged in the 1990s. The Soviet invasion of Afghanistan in late 1979 followed by a campaign to expel the invaders during the 1980s was one contributor to its development. Its global prominence increased following the events of 11th September 2001 when hijacked aircraft were flown into buildings in New York and Washington DC. The invasion of Iraq in 2003 further heightened tensions within the Middle East.

In this context Christians came under increasing pressure from the society they were part of with little action by their governments to provide due protection. Increasingly, the authorities granted impunity to perpetrators of anti-Christian violence. Leaders of recognised churches typically colluded with the political leaders, accepted being effectively confined to defined church property and supporting Christians only; religious registration became a tool to segregate society.

In mid 2013 the direction of political Islam became very unclear due to its failure and rejection in Egypt. President Morsi was removed from office by the Egyptian army acting in response to public protests involving the active participation of more than a third of the population.

In mid 2014 an armed group active in Syria since 2012 established territorial control of parts of Iraq, changed its name to 'The Islamic State' and declared the establishment of a Caliphate. The group called for all Sunni Muslims to pledge allegiance to this state. At the time of writing, this claim had not received formal recognition by any duly constituted national authority.

Study Guide

This additional material is included for those who wish, either alone or with others, to use the book as a tool for reflection or discussion. Much of the content is generally applicable, although some is specific to adherents of a particular religion – such material is duly marked.

The material is presented on a thematic basis with sections on: (a) the effects of religious registration on individuals and communities; (b) religion: lifestyle, worship and conversion; (c) the interactions amongst ethnicity, nationality and religion; (d) the Arab Awakening and the future of societies; and (e) the consistent rule of law applied equally to all.

A. The effects of religious registration on individuals and communities

Religious registration gives religion a prominent role within society since all are obliged to use religiously based personal status legal systems. What are the positive benefits of this? What possible negative consequences have we seen and how might they be mitigated? (e.g. see Lebanon, chapter 6, re the abuse of the system by some church leaders)

Considering those whose religious registration differs from their beliefs:

What are the effects on an individual's sense of identity?

What are the effects on immediate and wider family members?

What are the effects on those who desire a religious registration that is not recognised by their government? (e.g. Druze in Syria, Alevi in Turkey, Baha'i and atheists)

How do we respond when someone is obliged to change their registration in order to marry the person they love? How do we react when a country tells many of its female citizens that they cannot marry some of its male citizens? Do we approve of restrictions on who can marry whom? Or would we prefer that citizens should be freely able to marry someone from a different religious background? How should the religious registration of such couples be resolved, and what registration should their children be given? (see chapters 8, 15 and 22, for example)

How do we respond when a man refuses to register the birth of his children because he does not want their birth certificates to state a faith different from his own, or be raised in a different faith? (see Iraq, chapter 18, also Mohammed Hegazy, chapter 2)

How do we respond when the requests of the deceased are not respected? (see chapter 23)

What do we think of a legal system that allows an individual's legal personality to be removed, as happened to Ramzi and others in Jordan? (chapter 1) What do we think of a legal system that can be used in abusive ways by those seeking personal gain at the expense of relatives who hold a different religious registration from theirs? (e.g. Siham's estranged brother, chapter 1 and those claiming to be Meriam's relatives, chapter 11) Consider those who have chosen to follow a faith different from their religious registration (e.g. Ramzi). Should the jurisdiction of religious courts apply only when all those involved voluntarily accept their jurisdiction and judgements?

How do we respond to the linkages between religious registration and the topics of children's religious education and which religious bodies have, or can obtain, official recognition? Does the interdependency of the issues confuse us or excite us? Do we see it as a reflection of the interdependency upon which a healthy society flourishes?

Christians may wish to reflect on the patience and persistence displayed by those whose story of their confrontation with religiously motivated persecution we have read (e.g. Siham, chapter 1, the twins and their mother, chapter 2, Meriam, chapter 11, and pastor Yousef, chapter 12). What can Christians learn that enriches their religious belief and practices?

B. Religion: lifestyle, worship and conversion

How does one determine who is an adherent of a particular religion? What is the role of ethics, behaviour and attitudes, as well as religious belief and practice? What is the role of family and community? Who is qualified to make an assessment?

What comprises an appropriate lifestyle? Does a faith have to be lived out in order to mean anything? Many strands within Judaism, Christianity and Islam consider it should, asserting that religious belief that does not influence lifestyle is worthless. Some commentators suggest that the Israelites' Babylonian exile in the sixth century BCE (see appendix 1) implies that moral and ethical demands have priority over the holiness of place in the eyes of the God of Abraham. How many of us live accordingly?

Considering places of worship:

Do we value the places of worship that we have?

Do we welcome the stranger amongst us, including when we are worshipping publicly?

To what extent can we worship as we would like in unfamiliar settings, or in a location that is not officially designated as a place of worship?

How, if at all, do we identify with the Alevi in Turkey and Church leaders in Egypt, for example, seeking changes to the status quo concerning regulations and practices governing places of worship? (see chapters 5 and 17)

What in practice should equal treatment of places of worship involve? How should diversity within religions be handled, e.g. by multiple places of worship for specific strands, traditions or denominations? (see chapter 27)

How should the required number of places of worship be determined? What are the appropriate responsibilities of religious leaders and government officials? (see Turkey, chapter 5, Sudan, chapter 11 as well as Egypt, chapters 9 and 17)

What criteria are appropriate for religious bodies to acquire 'legal personality,' enabling them to own and operate places of worship?

Christians may wish to consider whether more churches should be granted the right to operate ecclesiastical courts? What is the optimum number of such institutions? (see Jordan, chapter 8, and Israel, chapter 14)

Considering religious conversion:

Do we respect the right of all to change their religion? (see for example Mohammed Hegazy, chapter 2, and the Gaza Strip, chapter 16)

We have described situations of families living as adherents of one faith at home but the children being treated as adherents of a different faith at school (see the twins, chapter 2, and North Africa, chapter 21). What are the effects on the families involved? What are the wider implications for society?

How might we advise someone wishing to change their religious registration to reflect their conversion knowing that to do so is likely to lead to discrimination? (e.g. in Turkey, chapter 5, and elsewhere)

What constitutes appropriate proselytising?

During our regional tour we encountered different models for changing religious registration. Consider the benefits and drawbacks of the following models:

the Lebanese model where the convert must obtain a letter of welcome from a duly authorised representative of the registration they wish to join

the Turkish model where the individual applies at any police station to change their registration

the Egyptian reconvert model that requires a birth certificate stating Christian and a letter from a duly recognised church confirming the reconversion the standard model that allows change of registration to Muslim but prevents change from Muslim to Christian or any other faith.

Do we respect those who choose to remain in situations of danger in order to maintain faithful witness for their faith? What price are we willing to pay to remain faithful to what we believe in? (see chapter 20)

C. The interactions amongst ethnicity, nationality & religion

During our regional tour we noted that all major faiths in the Middle East have considerable diversity. In what ways is it a strength and in what ways a weakness? Is diversity within a religion to be celebrated or lamented? How might intra-religion pluralism be affirmed and strengthened? How might doing so enrich society as a whole?

What are the advantages and disadvantages of regarding societies in the Middle East on religious, ethnic and tribal bases? Who constitutes a 'majority'? (see chapter 7)

Considering religion and the state:

What is the appropriate role of the state concerning religious entities?

Is the right of adherents of all religions, as well as those with no religious belief, to offer the ethical outworking of their beliefs as a contribution to public debate respected?

What should be the limits of the jurisdiction of religious courts? (see chapter 27)

Is it wise for a government – even a secular one – to overtly favour a strand of one religion over other strands of the same faith and other religions? (e.g. Turkey, chapter 5)

What are the benefits and costs of being a 'state religion'?

Where there is a state religion, why might it be in that religion's best interests to allow other religions and different strands of the same religion to flourish? (see chapter 26)

What are the implications of a government describing all citizens as Muslims irrespective of their religious beliefs and practices? (see chapters 21 and 22)

What are the effects of 'glass ceilings' based on religious registration?

How might governments demonstrate that they regard the Christians of the Middle East as a valued part of society? (see chapter 8)

Many countries in the Middle East have several religious registrations for Christians but have only one for

Muslims: what are the effects of this? Does this help or hinder the pluralism deficit? (E.g. Egypt, Iraq and Jordan recognise some of the diversity within Christianity whilst denying recognition of the diversity amongst Muslims; in contrast Lebanon officially recognises some of the diversity within Islam.)

How do we react when the Druze are regarded as a distinct religion (e.g. in Israel and Lebanon) and some Druze treat it as primarily an ethnic identification? In contrast, how do we think people feel when they are treated as part of Islam when they would prefer to have their distinctiveness recognised? (e.g. Druze in Syria, Alevi in Turkey, Yezidis in Iraq and others)

Should a civil personal status legal system be introduced to complement the religiously based systems? What are the potential benefits and drawbacks for religious bodies and society?

How do we respond to the Jordanian government's affirmation of Jordanian Christians' contribution to their country? (chapter 8) Is there a tension between this and its policies in public sector employment and its granting of authority to Islamic courts whose verdicts often prompt Christians to leave the country?

Muslims may wish to consider what it means to be an Islamic state as is claimed by Iran or a Muslim state as claimed by many countries in the Arab world. What effects does such identification have on citizens' lives, religious beliefs and practices, and sense of identity?

D. The Arab Awakening and the future of societies
(see chapter 10)

Do we identify with the prevalent calls to create greater dignity for all, provide more and better jobs, tackle corruption and give citizens a voice in how they are governed? Do we desire to see governance at local, municipal, regional, national and international levels that works for the benefit of all people?

How important is it to tackle corruption? How can corruption be reduced? What is the role of freedom of expression, opinion and the press in this area? How might greater freedom of religion contribute?

Considering pluralism:

Do we welcome and embrace the views and opinions of those different from ourselves? Do we embrace diversity?

How might societies throughout the Middle East become more pluralistic? How might religious leaders contribute to this?

Each of us might consider whether our attitudes and behaviours are truly pluralistic? What role do we see within each of our communities for promoting pluralistic practices?

How can constitutions be used to address the pluralism deficit and enable all parts of society to flourish? (see chapter 26) How might those involved in drafting constitutions resist the temptation and pressure to preserve the privileges of their core constituency to the detriment of wider society?

What effects does the linkage between religious registration and political representation have on the function of governance for the benefit of all? (see Lebanon, chapter 6, in particular, as well as Jordan, Egypt and Iraq, chapters 8, 9 and 18 respectively) Does it assist or hinder pluralistic approaches to governance?

Considering three countries in particular:

To what extent does Iraq illustrate the consequences of the pluralism deficit, predominantly in the face of Sunni-Shi'a and Arab-Kurd tensions, mistrust and some resorting to violence? How might the tensions between the federal government in Baghdad and the Kurdish Regional Government in Arbil be resolved? How do we respond to evidence of pluralistic governance being endorsed as seen in Kirkuk in 2014? (see Iraq, chapter 18)

Do we regard the Syrian crisis as a "civil war?" How do we assess the presence of foreign fighters and the involvement of numerous countries in supporting various parties to the conflict? (see Syria, chapter 19)

Readers in the West might consider calling upon our leaders to account for their actions, whilst acknowledging that there are few (if any) good policy options available.

How do we view Yemen's National Dialogue process? (see chapter 22) The inclusive process produced a clear proposal but the government at the time chose not to implement it. How might the outcome be implemented (as and when the armed conflict taking place at the time of writing comes to an end)?

How do we understand patronage? What are the positive benefits of seeking a patron? What might be regarded as negative consequences?

Christians might consider whether it is legitimate to view Jesus as the ultimate patron? E.g. Christianity teaches that Jesus is risen, ascended and seated at the right hand of God with access to all the resources of God and invites people to know him, trust him, let him guide and provide; he invites his followers to imitate him, to live as he did. Is this Christian discipleship?

E. The consistent rule of law applied equally to all

What are the consequences of the inconsistent application of law? In what ways does this impoverish society? How can justice be administered by the clear rule of law in an honour-shame culture?

In our regional tour we read several stories in which evidence was either not allowed or overlooked (e.g. Demiana, chapter 9, Meriam, chapter 11, and Hamid, chapter 12). In what ways are such practices honourable? How might trials in which religion is a factor be conducted according to best legal practice?

Do we seek to stand alongside those endeavouring to uphold their rights and their communities' rights? How do we enable others to articulate clearly the injustice that they face and wish to challenge? (see chapter 26)

Blasphemy laws, or to be more nuanced, the misapplication of blasphemy laws, are problematic in several countries. How might such laws be wisely codified, and what safeguards should be put in place to ensure the highest standards of legal processes are upheld?

Demiana's case concluded with her being exonerated but she was denied the right to return to the situation she held prior to being falsely accused. (see Demiana, chapter 9) What needs to change in society for such injustices to cease?

How do we understand 'reconciliation'? Does true reconciliation force the weaker party to accept whatever the stronger chooses to impose? Within the cultures of the Middle East, why are 'reconciliation meetings' given such weight when they have no basis in law and do not remove the state's duty to properly investigate criminal actions? (see Egypt, chapter 9; such practices occur elsewhere)

How do we react when a Supreme Court ruling is ignored with impunity by a religious body? What does the word 'supreme' mean? (see Israel, chapter 14) What is an appropriate balance between state and religious courts? How might current practices be amended to achieve such a balance?

How do we respond when those with no good, lawful options resort to illegal means? How might such legal systems be reviewed and amended? (see Egypt, chapter 9, noting that similar challenges arise elsewhere in the Middle East)

What do we think of the Iranian legal system's stipulation to consult the Supreme Leader's office for clarification on how Shari'a should be interpreted and applied? Does this ensure consistency or confer authoritarian power on the head of state? (see Iran, chapter 12)

How do we respond when laws criminalise acts that they fail to define adequately? What do we think of a government that places legal requirements on religious bodies and then fails to provide a mechanism by which they can be fulfilled? (see Algeria, chapter 21)

Do we agree that the actions of others, including those of nation states, should be subject to outside scrutiny? (see chapter 24) Do we long for mechanisms to prosecute those accused of committing genocide, war crimes and crimes against humanity to operate more quickly, effectively and widely, whilst upholding the highest standards of trial procedures? (see chapter 26)

Glossary

Al-Azhar: the leading academic institution within Sunni Islam; located in Cairo, Egypt; the head of al-Azhar also holds the post of Grand Mufti (see below) of Egypt

Al-Qaeda: a loosely connected network of armed groups

Alawite: an ethnic religious group with significant communities in Lebanon, Syria and Turkey; the religious aspect is regarded by some as part of Shi'a Islam and by others as a distinct religion outside of Islam

Alevi: a religious group primarily found in Turkey whose beliefs combine elements of Shi'a Islam and pre-Islamic Anatolian practices

Aliya: an ethnically Jewish person emigrating to Israel under the Israeli government's Right of Return law

Ansar Allah: a group originating in northwest Yemen, ethnically Houthi and religiously adherents of the Zaidism strand within Shi'a Islam

Apostasy: leaving Islam, defined here as having a religious registration of Muslim and choosing to become a follower of another religion or atheism

Apostate Jew: an ethically Jewish person who chooses to become an adherent of a religion other than Judaism

Arab: an ethnic group, historically originating in the Arabian Peninsula although migration has occurred for millennia

Arab Awakening: a socio-political phenomenon that arose in 2011 affecting most countries in the Middle East, North Africa and the Arabian Peninsula typified by protests calling for reform of governance structures, greater opportunity for all and recognition of the dignity and worth of all citizens; originally referred to as the Arab Spring

Arab League: a supra-national organisation whose membership includes the countries of the Arab world (see below) and a few closely related countries, including Djibouti and Somalia

Arab Spring: see Arab Awakening

Arab world: those countries located in the Middle East, North Africa and the Arabian Peninsula where Arabic is a national language (and the mother tongue of a majority of citizens); namely Algeria, Bahrain, Egypt, Iraq, Jordan, Kuwait, Lebanon, Libya, Mauritania, Morocco, Oman, Qatar, Palestine, Saudi Arabia, Sudan, Syria, Tunisia, United Arab Emirates (UAE) and Yemen

Armenian: an ethnic group; historically the first ethnic group to collectively become Christians

Ashkenazi: a strand within Judaism (see appendix 1 for origins)

Baha'i: a distinct religion that emerged out of Islam in the nineteenth century; its international headquarters are in Haifa, Israel

Berber: generic term for numerous distinct tribal groups indigenous to North Africa

Caliphate: a form of governance in Islam in which one person is both the political and religious leader

Catholic: a tradition within Christianity, most strands of which accept the authority of the Catholic Pope based in Vatican City in the state of the Holy See, a small state located within the city of Rome, Italy; Roman Catholicism is the most widespread branch of this Christian tradition

Cemevi: an Alevi place of worship

Chief Rabbinate: supreme authority within Judaism in Israel; has authority over personal status matters, kosher certification and other aspects of Judaism; the two Chief Rabbis (one Ashkenazi, one Sephardi) alternate the presidency

Daesh: the name used by many political and religious leaders in the Middle East for the group that declared itself 'The Islamic State' (see below); it is derived from an approximate acronym of the group's name in Arabic

Druze: an ethnic religious group present in Israel, Lebanon and Syria

Eastern Orthodox: a tradition within Christianity (see appendix 2 for origins); also referred to as the Chalcedon Churches

Eid al-Adha: Muslim festival celebrating Abraham's willingness to sacrifice his son in obedience to God – see Genesis 22:1-18 – noting that in the Islamic tradition it is Ishmael rather than Isaac who is to be sacrificed

Eid al-Fitr: three-day Muslim holiday marking the end of Ramadan (see below)

Family law: see Personal Status Law

Farsi: the national language of Iran; sometimes referred to as Persian

Fatwa: a religious ruling within Islam issued by a duly constituted religious authority

Glass ceiling: in employment, the denial of promotion beyond a certain level based on ethnic, religious, gender or other discriminatory grounds

Grand Mufti: the senior Islamic leader in a country

Haredi: a socio-religious community in Israel prioritising full-time religious study

Honour killing : the murder of a family member usually by a close relative motivated by the victim having brought shame on the family, or being perceived to have done so

Houthi: a tribe originating in northwest Yemen whose members are adherents of Zaidi Shi'a Islam; they have strived for autonomy within Yemen for many years (see also Ansar Allah)

Ismaili: a branch within Shi'a Islam; also known as the Sevener

Islamic State: an armed group that arose in Iraq before re-emerging in Syria; the group's original official title was *The Islamic State of Iraq and ash-Sham*; it is referred to as *The Islamic State in Iraq and Syria* (ISIS) and *The Islamic State in Iraq and the Levant* (ISIL) in some sources because the Arabic phrase Belad As-Sham can refer to Syria and also the entire Levant; the group re-titled itself *The Islamic State* in July 2014; the term Daesh (see above) is used by many in the Middle East

ISIS, ISIL: see Islamic State and Daesh

Jabhat al-Nusra: an armed group active in Syria that is affiliated to al-Qaeda

Karaiti: a strand within Judaism that accepts only Torah as definitive (see appendix 1 for its origins)

Kosher: conforming to Judaism's food laws

KRG: Kurdish Regional Government, i.e. the duly constituted body that governs three of Iraq's 18 provinces as an autonomous region within Iraq's federal structure

Kurd: an ethnic group with significant numbers in Iran, Iraq, Syria and Turkey who are commonly regarded as the largest ethnic group in the world without a state; there are seven distinct Kurdish dialects

Lausanne Treaty: of 1923, the founding document of the modern state of Turkey

Law of Return : Israel's law allowing those who are ethnically Jewish to emigrate to Israel

Legal personality: recognised in law, enabling the ownership of property, operation of bank accounts and signing of contracts; the common usage is in application to organisations and institutions; also applied to people who have reached the age of maturity, i.e. 18 in most countries

Levant: literally, the lands around Damascus; typically understood to mean modern day Iraq, Jordan, Lebanon and Syria; some usages including Israel, the West Bank and Gaza Strip

Mandean: a distinct religion, whose adherents are commonly described as being followers of John the Baptist; they originate in the southern Levant area but migrated to Mesopotamia early in the Common Era

Medhab: the tradition of Islamic legal jurisprudence that a Muslim follows; alternatively a school of Shari'a (see below)

Messianic believer: the term used by many ethnically Jewish people who accept Yeshua (the Hebrew form of Jesus) as the long-promised Messiah (see chapter 14)

Millet: a recognised religious order with authority from the state to operate a court system covering personal status law, handling matters such as marriage, divorce, custody of children, burial rites and inheritance

National Dialogue: a process in Yemen that took place from March 2013 to January 2014 involving tribal elders and representatives drawn from across Yemeni society, including women and youth, to discuss the future governance structure of the country

Oriental Orthodox: a tradition within Christianity (see appendix 2 for origins); also known as the Miaphysite/Monophysite Churches and the non-Chalcedon Churches

Orthodox Church: see Eastern Orthodox and Oriental Orthodox

Patron: one who provides resources and opportunities in return for loyalty

Personal status law: the legal framework in each country covering matters relating to an individual's status before the government such as marriage, divorce, custody of children, inheritance and burial rites

Peshmerga: the armed forces of the KRG (see above)

Pluralism: (a) the view that diverse groups can live together well in society by acknowledging and celebrating their ethnic, linguistic, religious and other differences (b) belief in the validity of a diversity of views and practices demonstrated by a conscious effort to understand each other's point of view

Protestant: a strand within Christianity originating in Europe during the Reformation and comprising numerous denominations

Ramadan: within Islam, a month of fasting during the hours of daylight

Reconvert: someone who converts from one religion to another and then reverts, or reconverts, back to their original religion

Reconciliation meeting : the practice in Egypt of holding a meeting involving those involved in an incident with the aim of restoring social harmony; such meetings have no standing in law and neither fulfil nor replace the state's duty to investigate any incident in which criminal acts have been perpetrated

Reform: a strand within Judaism that applies a critical review of Jewish law to determine appropriate ways of living in a modern age (see appendix 1 for its origins)

Salafist: a puritanical form of Sunni Islam with 'quiet', 'active' and 'jihadist' forms (see appendix 3)

Sephardi: a strand within Judaism (see appendix 1 for origins)

Shabak: an ethnic-religious group mostly located in the Sinjar district of Ninevah province, Iraq

Shari'a: Islamic jurisprudence or law; in its broadest understanding this covers all aspects of life including the daily prayer times as well as matters of criminal, civil and personal status law

Shi'a: a strand within Islam (see appendix 3 for origins)

Shi'ite: the adjective form of Shi'a

State party: a country that has ratified, or acceded to, an international treaty or covenant thereby committing to uphold the rights, duties and responsibilities described by the covenant or treaty

Sufism: a strand within Islam that emphasises purity of worship and inward mystical experiences of Islam;

occurs within both Sunni and Shi'a Islam; often involves an ascetic lifestyle

Sultan: ruler of the Ottoman Empire

Sunni: a strand within Islam (see appendix 3 for origins)

Taif Accord: treaty of 1989 that adjusted Lebanon's political system; crucial element in ending the Lebanese civil war

Torah: the first five books of the Hebrew Scriptures; also referred to as the books of Moses

Turkmen: an ethnic group that is part of the Turkic group of ethnicities; there are Turkmen communities in Iran, Iraq and Syria

Ward of the state: a child whose legal custody is held by the state; i.e. the parents no longer have legal custody, either because they have died or have been deemed unable or ineligible by the authorities to fulfil the duties of legal guardian

Wilayat-al-Faqih: literally, Guardianship of the Jurists; the theological basis within Shi'a Islam underpinning Iran's constitution following its 1979 revolution

Yeshua: the Hebrew form of Jesus

Yezidis: a Kurdish community whose distinct monotheistic religious beliefs are derived from Zoroastrianism and ancient Mesopotamian religions; most are located in northern Iraq with small numbers in Syria and amongst Kurdish diasporas

Zaidi: a strand within Shi'a Islam

Zoroastrianism: a monotheistic religion originating in Persia that appears in recorded history in the fifth century BCE

For Further Reading

Albright (2006): Madeleine Albright; *The Mighty and the Almighty*; MacMillan

Andrew (2004): Brother Andrew; *Light Force*; Hodder & Stoughton

Andrew & Janssen (2007): Brother Andrew & Al Janssen; *Secret Believers*; Hodder & Stoughton

Ashdown (2007): Paddy Ashdown; *Swords and Ploughshares*; Weidenfeld & Nicolson

Bowen (2013): Jeremy Bowen; *The Arab Uprisings – The People Want the Fall of the Regime*; Simon & Schuster

Boyd-MacMillan (2006): Ron Boyd-MacMillan; *Faith that Endures*; Sovereign World

Chakrabarti (2014): Shami Chakrabarti; *On Liberty*; Penguin Books

Chapman (2004): Colin Chapman; *Whose Holy City*; Lion

Dalrymple (1998): William Dalrymple; *From the Holy Mountain*; Harper Press

Evans (2008): Gareth Evans; *The Responsibility to Protect*; Brookings Institute

Garrison (2014): David Garrison; *A Wind in the House of Islam*; Wigtake

Horner (1989): Norman Horner; *A Guide to Christian Churches in the Middle East*; Mission Focus Publications

Musasher (2014): Marwan Muasher; *The Second Arab Awakening and the Battle for Pluralism*; Yale University Press

Parker (2001): Russ Parker; *Healing Wounded History*; D.L.T. Republished by SPCK in 2012

Riddell & Cotterell (2003): Peter Riddell & Peter Cotterell; *Islam in Conflict*; IVP

Ripken (2013): Nik Ripken; *The Insanity of God*; B&H Publishing

Rostampour & Amirizadeh (2013): Maryam Rostampour & Marziyeh Amirizadeh; *Captive in Iran*; Tyndale

Russell (2014): Gerald Russell; *Heirs to Forgotten Kingdoms*; Simon & Schuster

Said (2003): Edward Said; *Orientalism*; Penguin Modern Classic edition

Sennott (2003): Charles Sennott; *The Body and the Blood* (paperback edition); Public Affairs

Siddiqui (2013): Mona Siddiqui; *Christians, Muslims & Jesus*; Yale University Press

Wright (2015): James Wright; *The Martyrs of Malatya*; EP Books